The Complete Cheese Cookbook

A Benjamin Company/Rutledge Book

The World of Cheese

Cheese is a delicious, satisfying food that rates high marks
for nutrition as well. On the opposite page are pictured some
of the many kinds of cheese available—they are identified
in the sketch and list below. Turn to *The Romance of Cheese*
on page 81 for cheese lore and legend, information on the
manufacture of all kinds of cheese, helpful how-to-buy guides.

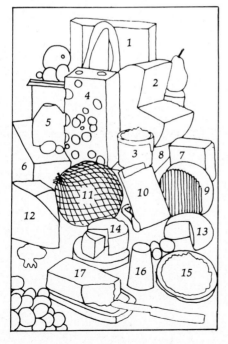

1. Cheddar
2. Blue
3. Ricotta
4. Swiss
5. Scamorze
6. Brick
7. Gjetost
8. Mozzarella
9. Edam
10. Colby
11. Provolette
12. Parmesan
13. Gouda
14. Camembert
15. Cottage
16. Sapsago
17. Cream

CONTENTS

A Word About This Book

Cheese, bread and wine have been on dining tables for as long as civilization has existed—indeed their development brought civilization with them. By accident and by design, the world's earliest cheese soon brought its particular blessing to the home. Cheese can be served as a simple snack or may grace the table of a gourmet.

Throughout the centuries and in many countries, men have experimented with producing limitless varieties of cheese, ranging from very soft and mild to very sharp and hard. Each has its own inimitable place in dining and in cookery.

As a pioneer in these developments, Kraft Foods has made important contributions to the world of cheese. Many of these will be brought out in this brand new book, *The Complete Cheese Cookbook*. You will also find valuable information on the various cheese families, their history and the care of cheese in the home.

The versatility of cheese is demonstrated in the many recipes created by the Kraft Kitchens' staff. You'll find new ideas, as well as some of the popular and traditional favorites that have appeared in commercials on the Kraft Music Hall. We hope this book will inspire you to further explore the wonderful world of cheese.

Dorothy Holland

Director, The Kraft Kitchens

To Start With

Served before a meal, at the beginning of a meal, standing by themselves as delicious snacks, these cheese-based appetizers will enhance your reputation as one who always serves something unusual—and unusually delicious.

Party Cheese Ball

2 8-ounce packages
Philadelphia Brand Cream
Cheese
2 cups (8 ounces) shredded
Cracker Barrel Brand Sharp
Natural Cheddar Cheese
1 tablespoon chopped pimiento
1 tablespoon chopped green
pepper
1 tablespoon finely chopped
onion
2 teaspoons Worcestershire
sauce
1 teaspoon lemon juice
Dash of cayenne
Dash of salt
Finely chopped pecans

Combine softened cream cheese
and Cheddar cheese, mixing until well blended. Add pimiento,
green pepper, onion, Worcestershire sauce, lemon juice and seasonings. Mix well. Chill. Shape
into a ball; roll in nuts.
Other ways: Roll in finely
chopped parsley or dried beef.

Full Moon Cheese Ball

1 3-ounce package
Philadelphia Brand Cream
Cheese
1 5-ounce jar Kraft Bacon
Pasteurized Process Cheese
Spread
1 5-ounce jar Kraft Pimento
Pasteurized Neufchatel
Cheese Spread
1 cup crushed canned
French-fried onions

Combine softened cream cheese
and cheese spreads, mixing until well blended. Stir in ½ cup
onions; chill. Shape into ball;
roll in remaining onions.

Parmesan Appetizer Log

1 8-ounce package
Philadelphia Brand Cream
Cheese
½ cup Kraft Grated Parmesan
Cheese
¼ teaspoon garlic salt
2 tablespoons finely chopped
green pepper
2 tablespoons finely chopped
pimiento
Chopped parsley

Combine softened cream cheese,
Parmesan cheese and garlic salt,
mixing until well blended. Add
green pepper and pimiento. Mix
well. Chill. Form into log shape
and roll in parsley.

"Philly" Crabmeat Spread

1 garlic clove, cut in half
1 8-ounce package
Philadelphia Brand Cream
Cheese
2 tablespoons milk
1½ cups (6½-ounce can)
crabmeat, drained, flaked
2 teaspoons lemon juice
Dash of salt and pepper
Dash of Tabasco sauce

Rub mixing bowl with garlic.
Combine softened cream cheese
and milk, mixing until well
blended. Add remaining ingredients; mix well. 1⅔ cups.

Triple Treat Spread

1 8-ounce package
Philadelphia Brand Cream
Cheese
¼ cup milk
2 cups (8 ounces) shredded
Cracker Barrel Brand Sharp
Natural Cheddar Cheese

* * *

2 slices crisply cooked
bacon, crumbled
1 tablespoon chopped green
onion

* * *

2 tablespoons Kraft Grated
Parmesan Cheese
1 tablespoon chopped parsley
1 tablespoon milk

* * *

1 tablespoon finely chopped
carrot
1 tablespoon finely chopped
celery
1 tablespoon finely chopped
green pepper
1 teaspoon finely chopped
onion

Combine softened cream cheese
with milk, mixing until well
blended. Add Cheddar cheese;
mix well. Divide mixture into
three portions, ⅔ cup each. To
one portion add bacon and
green onion. To second portion
add Parmesan cheese, parsley
and milk. To remaining mixture
add carrot, celery, green pepper
and onion. 2 cups.

Aloha Cheese Spread

1 8-ounce package
Philadelphia Brand Cream
Cheese
3 tablespoons Kraft Cold
Pack Blue Cheese
1 8¾-ounce can crushed
pineapple, drained
½ cup chopped pecans
1 teaspoon chopped candied
ginger

Combine softened cream cheese,
Blue cheese, pineapple, nuts and
ginger. Mix until well blended.
Garnish with coconut and pecan halves, if desired. 2 cups.

Cocktail Spread

1 8-ounce package
Philadelphia Brand Cream
Cheese
1 4-ounce package Kraft Cold
Pack Blue Cheese, crumbled
½ cup milk
1 cup (4 ounces) shredded
Cracker Barrel Brand Sharp
Natural Cheddar Cheese
1 teaspoon chopped chives
½ teaspoon Worcestershire
sauce

Combine softened cream cheese,
Blue cheese and milk, mixing
until well blended. Add Cheddar cheese, chives and Worcestershire sauce; mix well. 2½
cups.

Mock Paté

1 8-ounce package
Philadelphia Brand Cream
Cheese
1 8-ounce package liver
sausage
1 tablespoon chopped onion
1 teaspoon lemon juice
1 teaspoon Worcestershire
sauce
Dash of salt and pepper

Combine softened cream cheese
and liver sausage, mixing until
well blended. Add remaining ingredients; mix well. 2 cups.

Cheery Cheddar Spread

2 cups (8 ounces) shredded
Cracker Barrel Brand Sharp
Natural Cheddar Cheese
1/4 cup beer
2 tablespoons margarine
1/2 teaspoon prepared mustard
Dash of cayenne
1 tablespoon chopped chives
2 teaspoons chopped
pimiento

Combine cheese, beer, margarine, mustard and cayenne. Mix
until well blended. Stir in chives
and pimiento. 1¾ cups.

Potted Cheddar with Port

2 cups (8 ounces) shredded
Cracker Barrel Brand Sharp
Natural Cheddar Cheese
2 tablespoons soft margarine
2 tablespoons port
1/4 teaspoon paprika

Combine all ingredients; chill. 1
cup.

Zesty Cheese Spread

1 8-ounce package
Philadelphia Brand Cream
Cheese
1/4 cup salad dressing
1/3 cup chopped green pepper
1/4 cup chopped pimiento
2 tablespoons chopped onion

Combine softened cream cheese
and salad dressing; mix until
well blended. Add green pepper,
pimiento and onion; mix well.
1¾ cups.

Hot Beef Dip

1 cup (2½-ounce jar) dried
beef
1/4 cup chopped onion
1 tablespoon margarine
1 cup milk
1 8-ounce package
Philadelphia Brand Cream
Cheese, cubed
1/2 cup (3-ounce can) sliced
mushrooms, drained
1/4 cup Kraft Grated Parmesan
Cheese
2 tablespoons chopped
parsley

Rinse dried beef in hot water;
drain and chop. Cook onion in
margarine until tender. Stir in
milk and cream cheese, mixing
until well blended. Add dried
beef and remaining ingredients.
Mix well. Serve hot. 2 cups.

Mexicali Dip

1 pound Velveeta Pasteurized
Process Cheese Spread,
cubed
1 4-ounce can green
chilies, drained, chopped
2 cups (1-pound can) peeled
whole tomatoes, drained,
chopped
1 tablespoon dried minced
onion

Combine ingredients in saucepan; cook over low heat until Velveeta melts. Serve hot with corn or tortilla chips. 3 cups.

Caviar Dip

1 8-ounce package
Philadelphia Brand Cream
Cheese
1 cup dairy sour cream
¼ cup milk
1 2-ounce jar lumpfish
caviar
1 teaspoon grated onion

Combine all ingredients; chill. 2¼ cups.

"Philly" Guacamole Dip

1 8-ounce package
Philadelphia Brand Cream
Cheese
2 avocados, peeled, mashed
¼ cup finely chopped onion
1 tablespoon lemon juice
½ teaspoon salt
¼ teaspoon garlic salt
¼ teaspoon Tabasco sauce
1 cup diced peeled tomato

Combine softened cream cheese, avocado, onion and seasonings; mix well. Stir in tomato. Serve with corn chips or crisp tortillas. 4 cups.

Blue Cheese Dip

1 8-ounce package
Philadelphia Brand Cream
Cheese
⅓ cup milk
1 4-ounce package Kraft Cold
Pack Blue Cheese
2 tablespoons finely chopped
green pepper
2 tablespoons chopped
mushrooms

Combine softened cream cheese and milk. Add remaining ingredients; mix well. If chilled, remove from refrigerator at least 1 hour before serving. 1 cup.

Holiday Cheese Dip

1 8-ounce package
Philadelphia Brand Cream
Cheese
¼ cup milk
1 teaspoon anchovy paste
1 teaspoon paprika
1 teaspoon chopped chives
1 teaspoon capers

Combine softened cream cheese and remaining ingredients, mixing until well blended. Serve with crackers. 1¼ cups.

Opposite: Mexicali Dip

Mexican Bean Dip

*2 cups (1-pound can) baked
beans, sieved
1 8-ounce jar Cheez Whiz
Pasteurized Process Cheese
Spread
¼ cup catsup
1 teaspoon chili powder
Dash of Tabasco sauce*

Combine ingredients; heat.
Serve with corn chips or potato
chips. 3 cups.

Cheese Straws

*¼ cup margarine
2 cups (8 ounces) shredded
Cracker Barrel Brand Sharp
Natural Cheddar Cheese
1 teaspoon Worcestershire
sauce
¼ teaspoon salt
1 cup flour*

Heat oven to 375°. Thoroughly
blend margarine and cheese; stir
in Worcestershire sauce and
salt. Add flour; mix well. Roll
dough between two sheets of
waxed paper to ⅛-inch thickness; cut in 1 x 3-inch strips.
Place on lightly greased baking
sheet. Bake at 375°, 12 minutes.
3 dozen.
Another way: Cut dough in a
variety of shapes with small
cookie cutters.

Blue Cheese Meatballs

*2 pounds ground beef
1 4-ounce package Kraft Cold
Pack Blue Cheese
1 teaspoon salt
All purpose oil*

Combine ground beef, cheese
and salt; mix lightly. Shape into
1-inch balls. Brown in oil; cook
until done. 4½ to 5 dozen meatballs.

Sesame Seed Rounds

*¼ cup margarine
¼ cup Kraft Grated Parmesan
Cheese
2 tablespoons toasted sesame
seeds
18 2-inch bread rounds*

Heat oven to 325°. Combine
margarine, cheese and sesame
seeds; mix until well blended.
Spread on bread rounds. Bake at
325°, 15 minutes. 18 appetizers.

Hot Crabmeat Puffs

*1 8-ounce package
Philadelphia Brand Cream
Cheese
1 tablespoon milk
½ teaspoon cream-style
prepared horseradish
¼ teaspoon salt
Dash of pepper
1½ cups (6½-ounce can)
crabmeat, drained, flaked
⅓ cup slivered almonds,
toasted
2 tablespoons finely chopped
onion
Miniature Cream Puffs*

Heat oven to 375°. Combine softened cream cheese, milk, horseradish, salt and pepper. Mix until well blended. Stir in crabmeat, almonds and onion. Cut tops from Miniature Cream Puffs; fill with crab mixture. Replace tops. Bake at 375°, 10 minutes. 36 appetizers.

Miniature Cream Puffs

½ cup water
¼ cup margarine
½ cup flour
Dash of salt
2 eggs

Heat oven to 400°. Bring water and margarine to a boil. Add flour and salt; stir vigorously over low heat until mixture forms a ball. Remove from heat; add eggs, one at a time, beating until smooth after each addition. Drop teaspoonfuls of batter onto ungreased baking sheet. Bake at 400°, 30 to 35 minutes. Remove from baking sheet immediately.
Nice to know: These appetizers can be made ahead and frozen. Reheat at 375°, 30 minutes.

Beignets

¼ cup margarine
1 cup boiling water
1 cup flour
½ teaspoon salt
Dash of cayenne
3 eggs
2 cups (8 ounces) shredded Cracker Barrel Brand Sharp Natural Cheddar Cheese

Melt margarine in boiling water. Add flour, salt and cayenne; stir vigorously over low heat until mixture forms a ball. Remove from heat. Add eggs, one at a time, beating well after each addition. Stir in cheese. Drop by teaspoonfuls into hot oil, 350°. Fry until golden brown. 4½ to 5 dozen appetizers.

Appetizer Pinwheels

1 loaf unsliced sandwich bread
Kraft Whipped Cream Cheese with Pimento
Chopped parsley

Trim crusts from loaf. Cut into thin lengthwise slices. Spread slices with whipped cream cheese; sprinkle with parsley. Roll up, starting at narrow end. Wrap tightly; chill. Cut into ½-inch slices.

Sherried Cheese Rounds

1 5-ounce jar Old English Sharp Pasteurized Process Cheese Spread
1 tablespoon chopped parsley
2 teaspoons sherry
18 2-inch bread rounds, toasted

Combine cheese spread, parsley and sherry. Spread on toast rounds; broil until bubbly. Garnish with ripe olive slices, if desired. 18 appetizers.

A Fine Kettle of Soup

Hot soups to central-heat the family in cold weather,
chilled soups to cool off a summer dinner,
whole-meal soups for busy days—here are all kinds,
each one of them rich with the wonderful flavor of cheese.

Crème Vichyssoise

2 chicken bouillon cubes
4 cups boiling water
4 cups diced potatoes
¼ cup sliced onion
1½ teaspoons salt
1 8-ounce package Philadelphia Brand Cream Cheese
1 tablespoon finely chopped chives

Dissolve bouillon cubes in boiling water; add potatoes, onion and salt. Cover and simmer 20 minutes or until potatoes are very tender. Force mixture through sieve. Gradually add mixture to softened cream cheese, mixing until well blended. Add chives; chill. 8 servings.

Cheemato Soup

1 can condensed tomato soup
1¼ cups water
1 8-ounce jar Cheez Whiz Pasteurized Process Cheese Spread
Dash of pepper

Mix soup and water; heat. Add Cheez Whiz; stir until well blended. Add pepper; mix. 4 servings.

Golden Cream Soup

1½ cups boiling water
3 cups diced potatoes
½ cup chopped celery
¼ cup chopped onion
1 teaspoon parsley flakes
½ teaspoon salt
Dash of pepper
1 chicken bouillon cube
2 tablespoons flour
2 cups milk
½ pound Velveeta Pasteurized Process Cheese Spread, cubed

Add water to potatoes, celery, onion, parsley flakes, seasonings and bouillon cube. Cover; cook until tender. Blend flour with a small amount of milk; stir into vegetable mixture. Add remaining milk; cook until thickened. Add Velveeta; stir until melted. 6 to 8 servings.

Cheese 'n Ale Soup

⅔ cup shredded carrots
¼ cup chopped onion
¼ cup margarine
¼ cup flour
3 cups milk
2 cups (8 ounces) shredded Cracker Barrel Brand Sharp Natural Cheddar Cheese
½ cup ale or beer
Dash of salt and pepper

Cook carrots and onion in margarine until tender; blend in flour. Stir in milk; cook until thickened. Add cheese; stir until melted. Blend in ale or beer and seasonings; heat. 6 servings.

Old World Tomato Soup

4 slices bacon
½ cup sliced celery
¼ cup chopped onion
3½ cups (1-pound 12-ounce
can) tomatoes
1 can condensed
chicken broth
½ teaspoon salt
¼ teaspoon pepper
2 tablespoons cornstarch
¼ cup water
Kraft Grated Parmesan Cheese

Fry bacon until crisp; drain, reserving 2 tablespoons drippings. Cook celery and onion in bacon drippings. Add tomatoes, broth, seasonings, crumbled bacon and cornstarch combined with water. Simmer 15 minutes. Top each serving with Parmesan cheese. 6 servings.

Andean Potato Soup

2 chicken bouillon cubes
4 cups boiling water
4 cups diced potatoes
¼ cup sliced onion
2 teaspoons salt
½ teaspoon ground coriander
Dash of garlic powder
1 8-ounce package Philadelphia
Brand Cream Cheese
1 teaspoon parsley flakes
Dairy sour cream

Dissolve bouillon cubes in boiling water; add potatoes, onion, salt, coriander and garlic powder. Cover and simmer 20 minutes or until potatoes are very tender. Force mixture through sieve. Gradually add mixture to softened cream cheese, mixing until well blended. Add parsley; chill. When serving, garnish with sour cream, if desired. 8 servings.

Chili con Queso

1 pound ground beef
½ cup chopped onion
2 cups (1-pound can) kidney
beans, drained
2 cups (1-pound can) tomatoes,
undrained
1 8-ounce can tomato sauce
1 tablespoon chili powder
1 teaspoon salt
Cracker Barrel Brand Sharp
Natural Cheddar Cheese,
shredded

Brown meat; drain. Add onion; cook until tender. Stir in remaining ingredients except cheese. Cover and simmer 30 minutes, stirring occasionally. Top each serving with cheese. 6 servings.

Parmesan Corn Chowder

2 cups boiling water
2 cups diced potatoes
½ cup sliced carrots
½ cup sliced celery
¼ cup chopped onion
1½ teaspoons salt
¼ teaspoon pepper
¼ cup margarine
¼ cup flour
2 cups milk
1 cup (4 ounces) Kraft Grated
Parmesan Cheese
2 cups (1-pound can)
cream-style corn

Add water to potatoes, carrots, celery, onion, salt and pepper. Cover and simmer 10 minutes. Do not drain. Make white sauce with margarine, flour and milk. Add cheese; stir until melted. Add corn and undrained vegetables. Heat; do not boil. 6 to 8 servings.

Shrimp Cheese Chowder

2 cups thinly sliced onions
2 tablespoons margarine
2 tablespoons flour
1½ cups water
2 cups diced potatoes
1 cup sliced celery
1½ teaspoons salt
¼ teaspoon pepper
1 pound cooked shrimp
2 cups milk
2½ cups (10 ounces) shredded
Cracker Barrel Brand Sharp
Natural Cheddar Cheese
2 tablespoons sherry

Cook onions in margarine until tender; blend in flour. Stir in water, potatoes, celery and seasonings. Cover and simmer 20 minutes or until potatoes are tender. Add remaining ingredients; stir until cheese is melted. 6 to 8 servings.

Snow Scene Chowder

1 chicken bouillon cube
2 cups boiling water
2 cups diced potatoes
½ cup sliced carrots
½ cup sliced celery
¼ cup chopped onion
1½ teaspoons salt
¼ teaspoon pepper
¼ cup margarine
¼ cup flour
2 cups milk
2 cups (8 ounces) shredded
Cracker Barrel Brand Sharp
Natural Cheddar Cheese
1 cup diced cooked chicken

Dissolve bouillon cube in water; add vegetables and seasonings. Cover; simmer 10 minutes. Do not drain. Make white sauce with margarine, flour and milk. Add cheese; stir until melted. Add chicken and undrained vegetables. Heat; do not boil. 6 to 8 servings.

Cheddar Chowder

2 cups boiling water
2 cups diced potatoes
½ cup sliced carrots
½ cup sliced celery
¼ cup chopped onion
1½ teaspoons salt
¼ teaspoon pepper
¼ cup margarine
¼ cup flour
2 cups milk
2 cups (8 ounces) shredded
Cracker Barrel Brand Sharp
Natural Cheddar Cheese
1 cup cubed cooked ham

Add water to potatoes, carrots, celery, onion, salt and pepper. Cover; simmer 10 minutes. Do not drain. Make white sauce with margarine, flour and milk. Add cheese; stir until melted. Add ham and undrained vegetables. Heat; do not boil. 6 to 8 servings.

Other ways: Varsity Chowder —omit ham; add 8 slices crisply cooked, crumbled bacon. School Day Chowder—omit ham; add ½ pound sliced frankfurters. Midwest Chowder— omit ham; add 2 cups (1-pound can) cream-style corn.

Cape Anne Chowder

2 cups thinly sliced onions
2 tablespoons margarine
2 tablespoons flour
2 cups water
2 cups diced potatoes
1 cup sliced celery
1½ teaspoons salt
¼ teaspoon pepper
1 pound cod or haddock,
skinned, boned, cooked and
cut into pieces
1 7½-ounce can crabmeat,
drained, flaked
2 cups milk
2½ cups (10 ounces) shredded
Cracker Barrel Brand Sharp
Natural Cheddar Cheese

Cook onions in margarine until tender; blend in flour. Stir in water, potatoes, celery and seasonings. Cover and simmer 20 minutes or until potatoes are tender. Add remaining ingredients; stir until cheese is melted. 6 to 8 servings.

Lobster Bisque

¼ cup chopped onion
2 tablespoons margarine
1½ cups milk
1 8-ounce package Philadelphia
Brand Cream Cheese, cubed
1½ cups cubed cooked lobster
2 tablespoons sherry
¼ teaspoon salt

Cook onion in margarine until tender. Add milk and cream cheese. Cook, stirring occasionally, until cheese is melted. Add remaining ingredients; heat. 4 servings.

Say Cheese—and Meat

For most people—particularly the man in the family—meat
is the heart of the meal, and these meat-and-cheese
main dishes pair two favorites to produce inventive
dishes as high in body-building protein as they are savory.

Italian Pork Chops

8 pork chops, ½ inch thick
1 8-ounce can tomato sauce
¼ cup dry red wine
1 clove garlic, minced
1 teaspoon salt
¼ teaspoon pepper
¼ teaspoon oregano, crumbled
1 green pepper, cut in strips
1 3-ounce can sliced
mushrooms, drained
1 6-ounce package Kraft
Natural Low Moisture
Part-Skim Mozzarella Cheese
Slices, cut in half

Brown each pork chop on both sides in large skillet; drain. Combine tomato sauce, wine, garlic and seasonings; pour over meat. Add green pepper and mushrooms. Cover and simmer 30 minutes. Top each chop with cheese slice; cover until melted. 8 servings.

Ham Rolls Continental

6 slices boiled ham, ¼ inch
thick
Kraft Natural Swiss Cheese
Slices
1 10-ounce package frozen
broccoli spears, cooked,
drained
1 cup onion rings
2 tablespoons margarine
2 tablespoons flour
½ teaspoon salt
¼ teaspoon basil
Dash of pepper
1 cup milk

Heat oven to 350°. Top each ham slice with cheese slice and broccoli spears; roll. Secure with toothpicks. Place in 10 x 6-inch baking dish. Cook onion rings in margarine until tender; blend in flour and seasonings. Gradually add milk; stir until thickened. Pour over ham; cover baking dish with aluminum foil and bake at 350°, 25 minutes. 6 servings.

Veal Parmesan

6 veal cutlets (1½ pounds)
1 egg
½ teaspoon salt
¼ teaspoon pepper
½ cup dry bread crumbs
½ cup (2 ounces) Kraft Grated
Parmesan Cheese
2 tablespoons margarine
1 8-ounce can tomato sauce
¼ teaspoon basil
1 6-ounce package Kraft
Natural Low Moisture
Part-Skim Mozzarella Cheese
Slices, cut in half

Heat oven to 375°. Dip cutlets in combined egg and seasonings and then in mixture of bread crumbs and Parmesan cheese. Melt margarine in skillet; brown cutlets. Place cutlets in 12 x 8-inch baking dish. Combine tomato sauce and basil; pour over cutlets. Top each cutlet with slice of Mozzarella cheese. Bake at 375°, 30 minutes. 6 servings.

Parmesan Breaded Pork Chops

4 pork chops, ¾ inch thick
1 egg, beaten
1 teaspoon salt
¼ teaspoon pepper
⅓ cup Kraft Grated
Parmesan Cheese
⅓ cup dry bread crumbs
2 tablespoons all purpose oil

Heat oven to 350°. Dip pork chops in combined egg and seasonings and then in combined cheese and bread crumbs. Heat oil in skillet; brown each chop on both sides. Bake at 350°, 35 minutes, turning chops occasionally. 4 servings.

Meatloaf-in-the-Round

2 pounds ground beef
1½ cups (6 ounces) shredded
Cracker Barrel Brand Sharp
Natural Cheddar Cheese
2 cups fresh bread crumbs
1 egg
½ cup chopped celery
½ cup chopped onion
1 tablespoon Worcestershire
sauce
1 teaspoon salt
¼ teaspoon pepper
1 cup (8-ounce can) tomato
sauce

Heat oven to 350°. Combine meat, 1 cup cheese, bread crumbs, egg, celery, onion and seasonings; mix lightly. Shape into 9-inch round loaf in shallow baking dish. Bake at 350°, 1 hour; pour off drippings. Pour tomato sauce over meat; sprinkle with remaining cheese. Return to oven; continue baking 15 minutes. 8 servings.

Nice to know: This may be made ahead, covered and refrigerated overnight. Remove cover and bake as directed above.

Danish Cube Steak

¾ cup mayonnaise
1 4-ounce package Kraft Cold
Pack Blue Cheese, crumbled
¼ cup sliced green onion
6 cube steaks

Combine mayonnaise, cheese and onion; mix well. Reserve ½ cup mixture for topping. Spread one side of each steak with remaining mixture; fold in half. Broil on both sides until brown. Top with reserved mixture; broil until topping is lightly browned. 6 servings.

Skillet Supper

1½ pounds ground beef
1 cup (8-ounce can) tomato
sauce
½ cup chopped onion
½ cup dry bread crumbs
1 egg
1 tablespoon prepared
horseradish
1 teaspoon salt
Dash of pepper
1 8-ounce package Kraft
Pasteurized Process
American Cheese Slices

Heat oven to 350°. Combine meat, ½ cup tomato sauce and remaining ingredients except cheese; mix lightly. Spoon half of mixture into 8-inch skillet. Cover with 4 cheese slices and remaining meat mixture. Top with remaining tomato sauce. Bake at 350°, 40 minutes. Arrange remaining cheese slices on top; return to oven until cheese melts. 6 servings.

Matterhorn Meatloaf

1½ pounds ground beef
1½ cups fresh bread crumbs
1½ cups (6 ounces) shredded
Kraft Aged Natural
Swiss Cheese
1 cup milk
½ cup chopped onion
½ cup raisins
1 egg
1 teaspoon salt
¼ teaspoon pepper

Heat oven to 350°. Combine all ingredients except ½ cup cheese; mix lightly. Place mixture in 9 x 5-inch loaf pan. Bake at 350°, 1 hour and 30 minutes. Sprinkle with remaining cheese; return to oven until cheese melts. 6 to 8 servings.

Savory Meatball Supper

1 pound ground beef
¼ cup dry bread crumbs
1 egg, slightly beaten
½ teaspoon salt
½ teaspoon basil, crumbled ·
Dash of pepper
All purpose oil
1½ cups milk
1 8-ounce package Philadelphia
Brand Cream Cheese, cubed
¼ cup Kraft Grated Parmesan
Cheese
½ teaspoon onion salt
Hot cooked noodles

Combine ground beef, bread crumbs, egg, salt, ¼ teaspoon basil and pepper; mix well. Form into small meatballs. Brown in small amount of oil on all sides in skillet; drain. Heat milk and cream cheese over low heat, stirring until smooth. Add Parmesan cheese, onion salt and remaining ¼ teaspoon basil; mix well. Pour sauce over meatballs; simmer 10 minutes. Serve over hot noodles. 4 servings.

Dilly Meatloaf

2 pounds ground beef
1 cup fresh bread crumbs
⅓ cup catsup
⅓ cup chopped onion
⅓ cup chopped dill pickle
1 egg
1 teaspoon salt
¼ teaspoon pepper
* * *
Velveeta Sauce

Heat oven to 350°. Combine ingredients; mix lightly. Shape into loaf in shallow baking dish. Bake at 350°, 1 hour and 10 minutes. Serve with Velveeta Sauce. 8 servings.

Velveeta Sauce

½ pound Velveeta Pasteurized
Process Cheese Spread, cubed
¼ cup milk

Heat Velveeta with milk over low heat; stir until sauce is smooth.

Western Hash

1 pound ground beef
1 cup chopped green pepper
½ cup chopped onion
3½ cups (1-pound 12-ounce
can) tomatoes
1 cup uncooked rice
½ teaspoon salt
¼ teaspoon basil
Dash of pepper
½ pound Velveeta Pasteurized
Process Cheese Spread, sliced

Brown meat; drain. Add green pepper, onion, tomatoes, rice and seasonings. Cover and simmer 25 minutes. Top with Velveeta slices; heat until melted. 6 servings.

Meatballs Roma

½ cup chopped onion
2 tablespoons margarine
4 cups (2 1-pound cans)
tomatoes
1 6-ounce can tomato paste
½ teaspoon salt
½ teaspoon oregano
¼ teaspoon pepper
* * *

1 pound ground beef
Kraft Grated Parmesan Cheese
½ cup dry bread crumbs
2 eggs
½ teaspoon garlic salt
½ teaspoon salt
All purpose oil
Hot cooked spaghetti

Cook onion in margarine until tender. Add tomatoes, tomato paste and seasonings. Cover and simmer 30 minutes. Combine meat, ½ cup Parmesan cheese, bread crumbs, eggs and seasonings. Shape into 18 balls; brown in oil. Place meatballs in sauce; cover and continue cooking 30 minutes. Serve over spaghetti and top with additional Parmesan cheese. 4 to 6 servings.

Pleasin' Green Peppers

6 green peppers
1 pound ground beef
¼ cup chopped onion
1½ cups (12-ounce can)
whole kernel corn, drained
1 cup chopped tomato
¼ teaspoon salt
½ pound Velveeta Pasteurized
Process Cheese Spread, cubed

Heat oven to 350°. Remove tops and seeds from peppers; parboil 5 minutes. Drain. Brown meat with onion; drain. Add corn, tomato and salt. Stir in Velveeta, reserving ½ cup. Spoon mixture into peppers; top with reserved Velveeta. Place peppers in 12 x 8-inch baking dish; bake at 350°, 25 minutes. 6 servings.

Cheddar-filled Beef Rolls

1½ pounds ground beef
¼ cup dry bread crumbs
2 tablespoons barbecue sauce
1 egg
½ teaspoon salt
*   *   *
1 cup (4 ounces) shredded
Cracker Barrel Brand Sharp
Natural Cheddar Cheese
¼ cup dry bread crumbs
¼ cup chopped green pepper
2 tablespoons water

Combine meat, bread crumbs, barbecue sauce, egg and salt; mix well. Pat meat mixture into 14 x 8-inch rectangle on foil or waxed paper. Combine cheese, bread crumbs, green pepper and water; pat cheese mixture over

meat. Roll up jelly roll fashion, beginning at narrow end. Chill several hours or overnight. Heat oven to 350°. Slice meat roll into 6 servings. Bake in shallow pan at 350°, 25 to 30 minutes. 6 servings.

Suburbia Stew

2 pounds beef, cut in
1-inch cubes
All purpose oil
1 can condensed beef broth
1 cup water
2 teaspoons salt
¼ teaspoon pepper
1 bay leaf
6 medium onions, cut in
quarters
1½ cups sliced celery
6 medium carrots, cut in
thirds
*   *   *
½ cup (2 ounces) Kraft Grated
Parmesan Cheese
2 cups hot mashed potatoes

Brown meat in oil. Add beef broth, water and seasonings; cover and simmer 1 hour. Add vegetables and continue to simmer 30 minutes or until vegetables are tender. Pour into 10 x 6-inch baking dish. Stir cheese into potatoes; spoon on top of hot stew. Broil until potatoes are lightly browned. Sprinkle with additional cheese, if desired. 6 to 8 servings.

Quicker way: Two 1½-pound cans of canned stew may be used.

Opposite: Cheddar-filled Beef Rolls

Stroganoff Superb

*1 pound round steak, cut in
thin strips
3 tablespoons margarine
½ cup chopped onion
1 3-ounce can sliced
mushrooms, drained
½ teaspoon salt
¼ teaspoon dry mustard
¼ teaspoon pepper
1 8-ounce package Philadelphia
Brand Cream Cheese, cubed
⅔ cup milk
Hot parslied noodles*

Brown meat in margarine. Add onion, mushrooms and seasonings; cook until tender. Add cream cheese and milk; continue cooking, stirring until cheese melts. Serve over noodles. 4 servings.

Yankee Cheddar Steak

*1 pound round steak, ½ inch
thick
¼ cup flour
1 teaspoon salt
¼ teaspoon pepper
All purpose oil
1 medium onion, thinly sliced
1 8-ounce can tomato sauce
1 teaspoon garlic salt
1 cup (4 ounces) shredded
Cracker Barrel Brand Sharp
Natural Cheddar Cheese*

Heat oven to 350°. Cut steak in 4 pieces. Combine flour, salt and pepper; pound into steak. Brown in oil. Place in 12 x 8-inch baking dish; cover with onion and combined tomato sauce and garlic salt. Bake at 350°, 40 minutes. Sprinkle with cheese; return to oven until cheese melts. 4 servings.

Wellington Stew

*1½ pounds beef, cubed
¼ cup Italian-style dressing
3½ cups (1-pound 12-ounce
can) tomatoes
1 teaspoon salt
¼ teaspoon pepper
2 cups diced potatoes
1 cup sliced celery
12 small onions
Cheese Dumplings*

Brown meat slowly in dressing; add tomatoes and seasonings. Cover; simmer 1 hour. Add vegetables; cover and continue cooking 30 minutes. Drop dumplings by tablespoonfuls onto hot stew; cover and simmer 12 to 15 minutes. 6 servings.

Cheese Dumplings

*1 cup biscuit mix
⅓ cup milk
1½ cups (6 ounces) shredded
Cracker Barrel Brand Sharp
Natural Cheddar Cheese*

Combine biscuit mix and milk. Add cheese; mix well.

Say Cheese—and Poultry

Always delicious—and happily budget-minded—chicken and turkey take on new dimensions when they join with various kinds of cheese in delightful main dishes that are out of the ordinary and very good indeed.

Chicken Rococo

1 10-ounce stick Cracker Barrel
Brand Sharp Natural Cheddar
Cheese
4 chicken breasts, boned,
skinned
2 eggs, beaten
¾ cup dry bread crumbs
Margarine
1 chicken bouillon cube
1 cup boiling water
½ cup chopped onion
½ cup chopped green pepper
2 tablespoons flour
1 teaspoon salt
¼ teaspoon pepper
2 cups cooked white rice
1 cup cooked wild rice
1 3-ounce can sliced
mushrooms, drained

Heat oven to 400°. Cut cheese
into 8 equal sticks. Cut chicken
breasts in half; flatten each to
¼-inch thickness. Roll each
piece around stick of cheese;
secure with toothpicks. Dip in
eggs, then in bread crumbs.
Brown in margarine. Dissolve
bouillon cube in water. Cook
onion and green pepper in ⅓
cup margarine until tender; add
flour, seasonings and bouillon.
Cook until thickened. Add rice
and mushrooms; pour into 10
x 8-inch baking dish. Top with
chicken; bake at 400°, 20 minutes. 8 servings.

Chicken-in-the-Round

½ cup chopped onion
2 tablespoons margarine
1 can condensed cream of
mushroom soup
½ cup milk
⅓ cup mayonnaise
½ pound Velveeta Pasteurized
Process Cheese Spread, cubed
1 10-ounce package frozen
peas, cooked, drained
3 hard-cooked eggs, sliced
1½ cups chopped cooked
chicken
Cornbread Round

Cook onion in margarine until
tender. Blend in soup, milk and
mayonnaise; mix well. Add Velveeta, peas, eggs and chicken;
heat until Velveeta is melted.
Serve with Cornbread Round.
6 servings.

Cornbread Round

1½ cups cornmeal
½ cup flour
¼ cup sugar
4 teaspoons baking powder
1 teaspoon salt
2 eggs, beaten
1 cup milk
⅓ cup all purpose oil

Heat oven to 425°. Combine dry
ingredients. Add eggs, milk and
oil; stir until just blended. Pour
into well greased, heated 1½-
quart ring mold. Bake at 425°,
15 minutes.

Oven-fried Chicken Parmesan

*1 2½ to 3-pound broiler-
    fryer, cut up
1 egg, beaten
1 tablespoon milk
½ cup Kraft Grated Parmesan
    Cheese
¼ cup flour
1 teaspoon paprika
½ teaspoon salt
Dash of pepper
¼ cup margarine, melted*

Heat oven to 350°. Dip chicken in combined egg and milk, then in mixture of cheese, flour and seasonings. Place in 12 x 8-inch baking dish. Pour margarine over chicken; bake at 350°, 1 hour. 3 to 4 servings.

Alpine Chicken Casserole

*4 cups diced cooked chicken
2 cups sliced celery
2 cups toasted bread cubes
1 cup salad dressing
½ cup milk
¼ cup chopped onion
1 teaspoon salt
Dash of pepper
1 8-ounce package Kraft
Natural Swiss Cheese Slices,
    cut in thin strips
¼ cup slivered almonds,
    toasted*

Heat oven to 350°. Combine all ingredients except nuts. Pour into 2-quart casserole; sprinkle with nuts. Bake at 350°, 30 to 40 minutes. 6 servings.
Nice to know: This can be made

ahead, covered and refrigerated overnight. Bake, covered, at 350°, 50 minutes. Remove cover; continue baking 10 minutes.

Chicken Divan

*¼ cup margarine
¼ cup flour
2 cups milk
1 teaspoon salt
⅔ cup salad dressing
1 teaspoon Worcestershire
    sauce
¼ teaspoon nutmeg
2 10-ounce packages frozen
broccoli spears, cooked, drained
1 cup Kraft Grated Parmesan
    Cheese
4 large chicken breasts, cooked,
    sliced*

Heat oven to 350°. Make white sauce with margarine, flour, milk and salt. Add salad dressing, Worcestershire sauce and nutmeg; mix well. Arrange broccoli in 12 x 8-inch baking dish; sprinkle with ½ cup cheese. Cover with chicken; top with sauce and remaining cheese. Bake at 350°, 35 to 40 minutes. 4 to 6 servings.

Georgetown Chicken

½ cup milk
1 8-ounce package Philadelphia
Brand Cream Cheese, cubed
¼ cup Kraft Grated Parmesan
Cheese
½ teaspoon onion salt
1 cup chopped cooked chicken
1 3-ounce can sliced
mushrooms, drained
2 tablespoons slivered almonds
1 tablespoon chopped pimiento
1 10-ounce package frozen
asparagus spears, cooked,
drained
4 slices white bread, toasted

Heat milk and cream cheese
over low heat, stirring until
smooth. Add Parmesan cheese
and onion salt; mix well. Add
chicken, mushrooms, almonds
and pimiento; heat. Arrange
asparagus spears on toast; top
with sauce. 4 servings.

Chicken Valenciana

1 2½ to 3-pound broiler-fryer,
cut up
Salt and pepper
2 tablespoons all purpose oil
2 cups coarsely chopped onions
2 red or green peppers, cut in
strips
¼ pound ham, cut in thin
strips

2 garlic cloves, finely chopped
3½ cups (1-pound 12-ounce
can) tomatoes
⅔ cup (3 ounces) Kraft Grated
Parmesan Cheese
¼ cup flour
⅓ cup cold water
10 stuffed olives, cut in
half
10 pitted ripe olives, cut in
half
Hot cooked rice

Season chicken. Brown in oil in
10-inch skillet; remove. Add
onions, peppers, ham and garlic; cook until tender. Add tomatoes, ½ cup cheese and
chicken. Cover; simmer 25 to
30 minutes or until tender. Remove chicken to serving dish;
keep warm. Add combined
flour and water; cook, stirring
constantly until thickened. Add
olives, heat. Pour sauce over
chicken; sprinkle with remaining cheese. Serve with rice. 4 to
6 servings.

Baked Chicken Lucerne

3 tablespoons margarine
¼ cup flour
1 cup milk
1 chicken bouillon cube
½ cup boiling water
1 8-ounce package Kraft
Natural Swiss Cheese
Slices, cut in strips
¼ teaspoon dried tarragon
Dash of cayenne
4 large chicken breasts, cooked,
split
1 cup fresh bread crumbs
3 tablespoons margarine,
melted

Heat oven to 375°. Make white sauce with margarine, flour and milk. Dissolve bouillon cube in water; add to sauce. Add cheese and seasonings; stir until melted. Place chicken in a 10 x 6-inch baking dish; cover with sauce. Sprinkle with crumbs tossed with margarine. Bake at 375°, 20 to 25 minutes. 8 servings.

Chicken Kashmir

½ pound Tasty Brand Imitation
Pasteurized Process Cheese
Spread, cubed
½ cup skim milk
1 tablespoon chopped pimiento
¼ teaspoon curry powder
3 chicken breasts, boned,
halved and cooked
2 10-ounce packages frozen
broccoli spears, cooked,
drained

Combine Tasty Brand, milk, pimiento and curry powder. Stir over low heat until sauce is smooth. Arrange chicken breasts over broccoli on serving platter. Top with sauce. 4 to 6 servings.

Turkey Tetrazzini

¼ cup margarine
¼ cup flour
2 cups milk
1½ teaspoons salt
½ teaspoon celery salt
Dash of pepper
⅔ cup mayonnaise
1 7-ounce package spaghetti,
cooked, drained
2 cups chopped cooked turkey
½ cup cooked peas
2 tablespoons chopped
pimiento
½ cup Kraft Grated Parmesan
Cheese

Heat oven to 350°. Make white sauce with margarine, flour, milk and seasonings. Stir in mayonnaise. Add spaghetti, turkey, peas, pimiento and ⅓ cup cheese; mix lightly. Pour into 2-quart casserole; sprinkle with remaining cheese. Bake at 350°, 45 minutes. 6 servings.

Say Cheese—and Seafood

Start with fish from the can, from the supermarket, from the fish market or from your proud husband's own catch—add cheese and know-how and you'll produce main dishes that will have family and guests asking for seconds.

Capetown Dinner

¼ cup chopped onion
2 tablespoons margarine
1½ cups milk
1 8-ounce package Philadelphia
Brand Cream Cheese, cubed
1½ cups cubed cooked lobster
1 3-ounce can sliced
mushrooms, drained
¼ cup Kraft Grated
Parmesan Cheese
2 tablespoons chopped parsley
¼ teaspoon salt
Hot cooked rice

Cook onion in margarine until tender. Add milk and cream cheese. Cook, stirring occasionally, until cheese is melted. Add remaining ingredients; heat. Serve over rice. 4 to 6 servings.

Thermidor au Vin

¼ cup chopped onion
2 tablespoons margarine
1½ cups milk
1 8-ounce package Philadelphia
Brand Cream Cheese, cubed
1½ cups cubed cooked lobster
2 tablespoons sherry
1 3-ounce can sliced
mushrooms, drained
2 tablespoons chopped parsley
¼ teaspoon salt
White bread, toasted, cut in
triangles

Cook onion in margarine until tender. Add milk and cream cheese. Cook, stirring occasionally, until cheese is melted. Add lobster, sherry, mushrooms, parsley and salt; heat. Serve over toast. 4 to 6 servings.

Shrimp Superb

1 cup coarsely chopped
green pepper
⅓ cup Italian-style dressing
1 pound (2½ cups) cooked
shrimp
Kraft Grated Parmesan Cheese

Sauté green pepper in dressing. Combine shrimp and ¼ cup cheese; add to green pepper. Heat thoroughly. Sprinkle with additional cheese. 3 to 4 servings.

Saucy Shrimp Casserole

¼ cup margarine
¼ cup flour
2 cups milk
1 teaspoon salt
½ teaspoon Worcestershire
sauce
2 cups (8 ounces) shredded
Cracker Barrel Brand Sharp
Natural Cheddar Cheese
6 hard-cooked eggs, sliced
1 pound (2½ cups) cooked
shrimp

Heat oven to 350°. Make white sauce with margarine, flour, milk and seasonings. Add cheese; stir until melted. Add eggs and shrimp; mix lightly. Pour into 1½-quart casserole. Bake at 350°, 20 to 25 minutes. 6 servings.

Seville Shrimp

¾ cup margarine, melted
½ cup (2 ounces) Kraft Grated
    Parmesan Cheese
½ cup dry bread crumbs
⅓ cup chopped green onion
¼ cup lemon juice
1 garlic clove, minced
¼ teaspoon salt
1 pound cooked small shrimp

Heat oven to 350°. Combine margarine, cheese, bread crumbs, onion, lemon juice, garlic and salt; mix well. Add shrimp; mix lightly. Place mixture in four individual casseroles; bake at 350°, 20 to 25 minutes. 4 servings.

Fish Provençale

1 pound fish fillets
1 egg, beaten
1 tablespoon milk
½ cup dry bread crumbs
⅓ cup Kraft Grated
    Parmesan Cheese
¼ cup all purpose oil

Dip fish fillets in combined egg and milk, then in mixture of crumbs and cheese. Heat oil; cook fish on both sides until golden brown. 4 servings.

Newport Seafood Bake

2 tablespoons margarine
2 tablespoons flour
1½ cups milk
½ teaspoon salt
½ teaspoon celery salt
¼ teaspoon pepper
2 teaspoons chopped chives
2 cups (8 ounces) shredded
    Cracker Barrel Brand Sharp
    Natural Cheddar Cheese
1 pound cod or haddock
1 10-ounce package (3 cups)
    frozen shrimp, cooked
1 5-ounce can lobster,
    drained, cubed
2 tablespoons sherry
1½ cups fresh bread crumbs
3 tablespoons margarine,
    melted

Heat oven to 350°. Make white sauce with margarine, flour, milk and seasonings. Add cheese, stirring until melted. Cook fish; skin, bone and cut in pieces. Add fish, shrimp, lobster and sherry to sauce; pour into 2-quart casserole. Toss crumbs with margarine; sprinkle on top of casserole. Bake at 350°, 25 minutes. 6 to 8 servings.

41

Fisherman's Stew

*1 pound fresh or frozen red
snapper, mullet or redfish
fillets
1 pound fresh or frozen
raw shrimp
1 dozen fresh or frozen clams
1 cup coarsely chopped onion
1 clove garlic, minced
¼ cup margarine
2 cups coarsely chopped
fresh tomato
2 cans condensed
beef broth
½ cup sherry
4 lemon slices
2 teaspoons salt
3 whole allspice
1 small bay leaf
Dash of cayenne
Dash of thyme
Kraft Grated Parmesan Cheese*

Thaw frozen fish and skin fillets. Cut in slices or large chunks. Thaw frozen shrimp; peel and devein. Thaw frozen clams; clean. Sauté onion and garlic in margarine in large saucepan until tender. Add tomato, beef broth, sherry, lemon and seasonings; simmer gently, uncovered, 30 minutes. Add fish, shrimp and clams;

simmer 15 to 20 minutes or until fish flakes easily and clams open. Top each serving with cheese. 4 to 6 servings.

Halibut with Lobster Sauce

*½ cup dry bread crumbs
2 tablespoons Kraft
Grated Parmesan Cheese
6 ½-pound halibut steaks
¼ cup margarine, melted
* * **

*2 tablespoons margarine
2 tablespoons flour
1 cup milk
¼ teaspoon salt
1 7½-ounce can lobster,
drained, cut in chunks
2 tablespoons chopped green
onion
2 tablespoons chopped parsley
¼ cup Kraft Grated
Parmesan Cheese
1 tablespoon sherry*

Heat oven to 400°. Combine crumbs and cheese. Brush halibut with margarine; coat with crumbs. Place in greased 12 x 8-inch baking dish. Bake at 400°, 15 minutes or until fish flakes easily. Make white sauce with margarine, flour, milk and salt. Add lobster, onion and parsley; heat thoroughly. Stir in cheese and sherry. Heat. Serve over fish. 6 servings.

Gloucester Halibut

2 12-ounce packages frozen
    halibut steaks, thawed
    Salt and pepper
¼ cup margarine, melted
1 tablespoon lemon juice
    "Philly" Tartar Sauce

Heat oven to 350°. Sprinkle fish
with salt and pepper. Place in
well greased 12 x 8-inch baking
dish. Combine margarine and
lemon juice; pour over fish.
Bake at 350°, 25 minutes. Serve
with "Philly" Tartar Sauce. 4
to 6 servings.

"Philly" Tartar Sauce

1 8-ounce package Philadelphia
    Brand Cream Cheese
⅓ cup mayonnaise
2 tablespoons milk
2 teaspoons sweet pickle relish
1 teaspoon finely chopped
    onion
½ teaspoon chopped capers

Combine softened cream cheese
and remaining ingredients; mix
well. 1½ cups.

Scallops Palermo

2 12-ounce packages frozen
    scallops, thawed, drained
⅔ cup dry bread crumbs
½ cup Kraft Grated
    Parmesan Cheese
2 eggs, beaten
All purpose oil

Roll scallops in combined bread
crumbs and cheese, dip in egg
and roll again in bread crumb

mixture. Heat oil in skillet; fry
scallops until golden brown. 6
servings.

Rainbow Tuna

½ pound Tasty Brand Imitation
    Pasteurized Process Cheese
    Spread, cubed
½ cup skim milk
1 7-ounce can water-pack
    tuna, drained, flaked
¼ cup chopped onion
2 tablespoons chopped
    pimiento
1 10-ounce package frozen
    asparagus spears, cooked,
    drained
4 slices white bread, toasted

Combine Tasty Brand and milk;
stir over low heat until sauce is
smooth. Add tuna, onion and
pimiento. Arrange asparagus
spears on toast; top with sauce.
4 servings.

Maritime Burgers

1 13½-ounce can water-pack
    tuna, drained, flaked
2 eggs, slightly beaten
¾ cup skim milk
¼ cup dry bread crumbs
¼ cup chopped green pepper
2 tablespoons chopped onion
4 tomato slices
½ pound Tasty Brand Imitation
    Pasteurized Process Cheese
    Spread, cubed
1 teaspoon lemon juice
¼ teaspoon dill weed

Heat oven to 375°. Combine tuna, eggs, ¼ cup milk, bread crumbs, green pepper and onion. Shape into 4 patties. Place on greased baking sheet; bake at 375°, 15 minutes. Remove patties from oven; top each with tomato slice and return to oven 5 minutes. Combine Tasty Brand, remaining ½ cup milk, lemon juice and dill weed. Stir over low heat until sauce is smooth; serve over tuna patties. 4 servings.

Heat oven to 350°. Make white sauce with margarine, flour and milk. Add remaining ingredients except sauce; mix well. Shape into loaf. Bake in shallow pan at 350°, 1 hour. Serve with Velveeta Sauce. 6 to 8 servings.

Velveeta Sauce

½ pound Velveeta Pasteurized Process Cheese Spread, cubed
¼ cup milk

Heat Velveeta with milk over low heat, stirring until sauce is smooth. 1 cup.

Puget Sound Supper

2 tablespoons margarine
2 tablespoons flour
1 cup milk
1 1-pound can salmon, drained, flaked
½ cup salad dressing
1 egg, beaten
1 cup dry bread crumbs
½ cup chopped celery
½ cup chopped onion
¼ cup chopped green pepper
1 tablespoon lemon juice
1 teaspoon salt
Velveeta Sauce

Wonderful Cheese Dress-ups

A vegetable can be a dreary thing (poll the children if
you don't go along with that opinion); cheese not
only adds protein to vegetables and side dishes,
but taste punch as well, making them welcome at any meal.

Garden Vegetable Medley

*½ pound Velveeta Pasteurized
Process Cheese Spread, cubed
¼ cup milk
Dash of cayenne
1 head cauliflower, cooked
2 cups whole green beans,
cooked
2 cups sliced carrots, cooked*

Heat Velveeta and milk over low heat; add cayenne. Stir until sauce is smooth. Arrange hot vegetables on platter; pour sauce over vegetables. 6 to 8 servings.

Fiesta Corn

*½ cup chopped onion
2 tablespoons margarine
2 tablespoons flour
¼ pound Velveeta Pasteurized
Process Cheese Spread, cubed
2 cups diced fresh tomatoes
2 cups (1-pound can) whole
kernel corn, drained
½ teaspoon salt
Dash of pepper*

Cook onion in margarine; blend in flour. Stir in Velveeta and tomatoes; cook until Velveeta is melted. Add corn and seasonings; continue cooking 5 minutes, stirring occasionally. 6 to 8 servings.

Chilean Corn Casserole

*2 1-pound 1-ounce cans
cream-style corn
⅓ cup Kraft Grated
Parmesan Cheese
4 slices crisply cooked
bacon, crumbled
Tangy Tomato Relish*

Heat oven to 350°. Combine corn, cheese and bacon; mix well. Pour into 1-quart casserole; bake at 350°, 35 minutes. Serve with Tangy Tomato Relish. 8 servings.

Tangy Tomato Relish

*2 cups diced tomatoes
¾ cup chopped onion
1 tablespoon chopped parsley
1 tablespoon finely chopped
green chili pepper
1 tablespoon lemon juice
Dash of garlic powder*

Combine all ingredients; mix lightly. 2 cups.

Saucy Vegetables

*½ pound Velveeta Pasteurized
Process Cheese Spread, cubed
¼ cup milk
2 cups (1-pound can) cut green
beans, drained
2 cups (1-pound can) sliced
carrots, drained
1 cup French-fried onions*

Combine Velveeta and milk in saucepan over low heat; stir until sauce is smooth. Add green beans and carrots; heat. Pour into serving dish; top with onions. 4 servings.

Gala Green Beans

*2 slices bacon
1 cup onion rings
¼ cup Kraft Grated Parmesan
Cheese
1 9-ounce package frozen
whole green beans, cooked,
drained*

Cook bacon until crisp. Remove from skillet; crumble. Cook onion rings in bacon fat until tender. Toss onions and cheese with hot green beans; sprinkle with bacon. 4 servings.

Swiss Souffléed Beans

*½ cup chopped onion
2 tablespoons margarine
2 eggs, beaten
¼ cup milk
1 teaspoon salt
¼ teaspoon pepper
1 10-ounce package frozen cut
green beans, cooked, drained
1 cup (4 ounces) shredded Kraft
Aged Natural Swiss Cheese*

Cook onion in margarine in 8-inch skillet until tender. Stir in remaining ingredients; cover and cook over low heat 15 minutes. Cut into wedges; serve immediately. 6 servings.

Golden Green Beans

*½ pound Velveeta Pasteurized
Process Cheese Spread, cubed
6 slices crisply cooked
bacon, crumbled
1 tablespoon finely chopped
onion
2 10-ounce packages frozen cut
green beans, cooked, drained*

Heat oven to 350°. Add Velveeta, bacon and onion to beans; mix lightly. Place in 1-quart casserole; bake at 350°, 10 minutes. Stir well before serving. 6 to 8 servings.

Dilly Green Beans

*4 cups fresh cut green beans
or 2 10-ounce packages
frozen cut green beans
2 tablespoons chopped onion
¼ teaspoon dill weed
½ pound Velveeta Pasteurized
Process Cheese Spread, cubed
¼ cup croutons*

Heat oven to 350°. Cook beans with onion and dill weed; drain. Add Velveeta; mix lightly. Place in 1-quart casserole; top with croutons. Bake at 350°, 12 to 15 minutes. 6 to 8 servings.

Great Green Beans

*4 cups cut green beans, cooked,
drained
1 4-ounce container Kraft
Whipped Cream Cheese with
Bacon and Horseradish*

Combine hot beans and whipped cream cheese; stir until blended. 6 servings.

Country Carrots

*3 cups sliced carrots,
cooked, drained
1 4-ounce container Kraft
Whipped Cream Cheese
with Chives*

Combine hot carrots and whipped cream cheese; stir until blended. 4 to 6 servings.

Asparagus Special

*1 4-ounce container Kraft
Whipped Cream Cheese
with Roquefort
¼ cup milk
1 10-ounce package frozen
asparagus spears, cooked,
drained*

Combine whipped cream cheese and milk. Heat, stirring until smooth. Pour over asparagus spears; sprinkle with paprika, if desired. 4 servings.

Asparagus Delmonico

*½ cup milk
1 8-ounce package Philadelphia
Brand Cream Cheese, cubed
¼ cup (2 ounces) Kraft Cold
Pack Blue Cheese, crumbled
Dash of onion salt
2 10-ounce packages frozen
asparagus spears, cooked,
drained*

Heat milk and cream cheese over low heat, stirring until smooth. Blend in remaining ingredients except asparagus. Serve over hot asparagus. Top with additional Blue cheese, if desired. 4 to 6 servings.

Sovereign Onions

*8 medium onions, peeled
½ cup chopped tomato
¼ cup margarine
1 cup fresh bread crumbs
1 5-ounce jar Kraft Bacon
Pasteurized Process Cheese
Spread
½ teaspoon salt
Dash of pepper*

Heat oven to 350°. Cook onions in boiling water 15 minutes; drain. Cool. Scoop out centers of onions, leaving ½-inch shell. Chop onion removed from center. Cook onion and tomato in margarine until tender. Add bread crumbs, cheese spread and seasonings; mix well. Fill onion shells; bake at 350°, 35 to 40 minutes. 8 servings.

Pleasin' Peas

1 10-ounce package frozen
peas, cooked, drained
1 4-ounce container Kraft
Whipped Cream Cheese with
Chives
1 tablespoon milk

Combine hot peas, whipped
cream cheese and milk; stir until blended. 4 servings.

Golden Baked Peppers

3 green peppers, cut in half
1 5-ounce jar Old English
Sharp Pasteurized Process
Cheese Spread
1 ¾ cups (1-pound 1-ounce
can) whole kernel corn,
drained
1 tomato, chopped
1 cup fresh bread crumbs
2 tablespoons margarine,
melted

Heat oven to 350°. Remove
seeds from peppers; parboil 5
minutes. Drain. Heat cheese
spread in saucepan over low
heat; stir in corn and tomato.
Fill peppers. Top with crumbs
tossed with margarine; bake at
350°, 30 to 35 minutes. 6 servings.

Perky Peas 'n Potatoes

¾ cup milk
1 8-ounce package Philadelphia
Brand Cream Cheese, cubed
¼ cup Kraft Grated Parmesan
Cheese
½ teaspoon onion salt
1 1-pound can small whole
potatoes, heated, drained
1 10-ounce package frozen
peas, cooked, drained

Heat milk and cream cheese
over low heat, stirring until
smooth. Add Parmesan cheese
and onion salt; mix well. Add
vegetables. Pour into serving
dish; sprinkle with additional
Parmesan cheese, if desired. 6
servings.

Piquant Broccoli

1 8-ounce package Philadelphia
Brand Cream Cheese
¼ cup salad dressing
¼ cup milk
⅓ cup chopped green pepper
¼ cup chopped pimiento
2 tablespoons chopped onion
2 10-ounce packages frozen
broccoli spears, cooked,
drained

Combine softened cream
cheese, salad dressing and milk;
mix well. Add green pepper, pimiento and onion; mix well.
Heat over low heat. Serve over
broccoli. 4 to 6 servings.

Tomatoes Continental

6 medium tomatoes
1 cup fresh bread crumbs
¼ cup margarine, melted
Kraft Grated Parmesan Cheese
1 10-ounce package frozen
peas, thawed

Heat oven to 350°. Remove tops of tomatoes; hollow out centers. Combine bread crumbs, margarine and ¼ cup cheese; toss with peas. Fill tomatoes. Place in 10 x 6-inch baking dish; bake at 350°, 25 to 30 minutes. Sprinkle with additional cheese, if desired. 6 servings.

Savory Spinach Casserole

1 8-ounce package Philadelphia
Brand Cream Cheese
¼ cup milk
2 10-ounce packages frozen
chopped spinach, cooked,
drained
⅓ cup Kraft Grated
Parmesan Cheese

Heat oven to 350°. Combine softened cream cheese and milk; mix well. Place spinach in 1-quart casserole; top with cream cheese mixture. Sprinkle with Parmesan cheese. Bake at 350°, 20 minutes. 4 to 6 servings.

Zesty Zucchini

2 pounds zucchini, sliced
⅓ cup chopped onion
Margarine
2 tablespoons flour
½ cup milk
½ teaspoon salt
½ pound Velveeta Pasteurized
Process Cheese Spread, cubed
2 medium tomatoes, chopped
1½ cups fresh bread crumbs
3 tablespoons margarine,
melted

Heat oven to 350°. Cook zucchini and onion in ¼ cup margarine over medium heat for 5 minutes. Make white sauce with 2 tablespoons margarine, flour, milk and salt. Add Velveeta; stir until melted. Layer half of zucchini mixture, tomatoes and Velveeta sauce in 12 x 8-inch baking dish; repeat layers. Top with crumbs tossed with melted margarine; bake at 350°, 35 minutes. 8 servings.

Creamy Potato Puff

1 8-ounce package Philadelphia
Brand Cream Cheese
4 cups hot mashed potatoes
1 egg, beaten
⅓ cup finely chopped onion
¼ cup chopped pimiento
1 teaspoon salt
Dash of pepper

Heat oven to 350°. Combine softened cream cheese and potatoes, mixing until well blended. Add remaining ingredients; place in 1-quart casserole. Bake at 350°, 45 minutes. 6 to 8 servings.

Other ways: Substitute chopped green pepper for onion or sprinkle with crisply cooked crumbled bacon.

Zucchini Bake

6 medium zucchini
½ cup chopped onion
2 tablespoons margarine
1 cup chopped tomato
1 teaspoon salt
¼ teaspoon poultry seasoning
Dash of pepper
1½ cups (6 ounces) shredded
Cracker Barrel Brand Sharp
Natural Cheddar Cheese
4 slices crisply cooked
bacon, crumbled

Heat oven to 350°. Trim ends of zucchini. Cook, covered, in boiling salted water 5 to 8 minutes; drain. Cut in half lengthwise. Scoop out centers; chop. Cook onion in margarine until tender; combine with chopped zucchini, tomato, seasonings, cheese and bacon. Fill zucchini. Arrange in 13 x 9-inch baking pan. Bake at 350°, 30 minutes. 6 servings.

Sunny Scalloped Potatoes

5 cups sliced potatoes
2 tablespoons flour
1 teaspoon salt
Dash of pepper
½ pound Velveeta Pasteurized
Process Cheese Spread, cubed
¾ cup milk
¼ cup chopped green pepper
¼ cup chopped onion
2 tablespoons pimiento strips

Heat oven to 350°. Coat potatoes with combined flour and seasonings. Place in 12 x 8-inch baking dish. Heat Velveeta and milk over low heat; add green pepper, onion and pimiento. Pour Velveeta sauce over potatoes. Bake at 350°, 50 minutes or until potatoes are done. 4 to 6 servings.

Cheese Risotto

1 cup chopped onion
3 tablespoons margarine
1 cup uncooked rice
2 cups water
2 chicken bouillon cubes
1 3-ounce can sliced
mushrooms, undrained
½ teaspoon salt
Dash of pepper
1½ cups (6 ounces) shredded
Cracker Barrel Brand Sharp
Natural Cheddar Cheese

Heat oven to 350°. Cook onion in margarine until tender. Stir in rice; cook until lightly browned. Add remaining ingredients except cheese. Bring to a boil; simmer 5 minutes. Layer rice mixture and 1 cup cheese in 1½-quart casserole. Bake, covered, at 350°, 1 hour. Sprinkle with remaining cheese; return to oven until cheese melts. 6 to 8 servings.

Double-Treat Baked Potatoes

Baked potatoes
Margarine
Milk
Kraft Bacon Pasteurized
Process Cheese Spread
Salt and pepper

Heat oven to 375°. Slice tops from baked potatoes; scoop out insides. For each potato, add 1 tablespoon margarine, 1 tablespoon milk and 2 tablespoons cheese spread. Mix until well blended; season to taste. Fill shells; place on baking sheet. Bake at 375°, 20 minutes or until lightly browned.

One-Dish Meals

One-dish wonders, these should be called—here is a
collection of casserole and skillet concoctions that will
be favorites with your family from the first day you
make them—and, as a bonus, save you hours of kitchen time.

Devonshire Spaghetti

½ cup chopped onion
½ cup chopped green pepper
2 tablespoons margarine
2 cups (1-pound can) tomatoes
½ teaspoon salt
¼ teaspoon pepper
1 7-ounce package spaghetti,
cooked, drained
1 cup diced cooked chicken
1 cup cooked ham strips
Velveeta Pasteurized Process
Cheese Spread

Heat oven to 350°. Cook onion and green pepper in margarine until tender. Stir in tomatoes and seasonings. Add spaghetti, chicken, ham and ½ pound cubed Velveeta; mix well. Pour into 2-quart casserole; bake at 350°, 25 minutes. Top with Velveeta slices; return to oven until Velveeta melts. 6 to 8 servings.

Country Chicken Casserole

1 cup milk
½ cup salad dressing
1 pound Velveeta Pasteurized
Process Cheese Spread, cubed
2 cups cubed cooked chicken
1 10-ounce package frozen
peas and carrots, cooked,
drained
5 ounces spaghetti, cooked,
drained
1 tablespoon chopped chives

Heat oven to 350°. Combine milk and salad dressing; add Velveeta. Heat over low heat, stirring until sauce is smooth. Add remaining ingredients; mix well. Pour into 2-quart casserole; bake at 350°, 35 to 40 minutes. 6 to 8 servings.

Country Fare Casserole

1¼ cups water
½ cup uncooked rice
1 cup cubed cooked ham
½ pound Velveeta Pasteurized
Process Cheese Spread, cubed
1 10-ounce package frozen
peas, thawed
6 hard-cooked eggs, sliced
⅓ cup chopped onion
¼ cup chopped pimiento
¼ cup milk
½ teaspoon salt

Bring water to boil; add rice. Cover and simmer 10 minutes; add remaining ingredients. Cover and continue cooking 20 minutes or until rice is done. 6 to 8 servings.

Blue Ribbon Ham Casserole

½ pound Velveeta Pasteurized
Process Cheese Spread, cubed
½ cup milk
3 cups diced cooked potatoes
¾ cup cubed cooked ham
6 hard-cooked eggs, sliced
¼ cup chopped green pepper
½ teaspoon salt

Heat Velveeta with milk over low heat; stir until sauce is smooth. Add remaining ingredients; mix well. Heat thoroughly, stirring occasionally. 6 servings.

Ham Apollo

1/4 cup chopped onion
2 tablespoons margarine
2 tablespoons flour
1/2 teaspoon salt
Dash of pepper
1 1/2 cups milk
1 cup diced cooked ham
Kraft Grated Parmesan Cheese
2 cups (4 ounces) green
noodles, cooked, drained

Heat oven to 350°. Cook onion in margarine until tender; blend in flour and seasonings. Gradually add milk, stirring until thickened. Stir in ham and 1/2 cup cheese. Alternate layers of noodles and sauce in 1-quart casserole; top with additional cheese. Bake at 350°, 20 minutes. 4 to 6 servings.

Heritage Supper

2 tablespoons margarine
2 tablespoons flour
2 cups milk
1/4 teaspoon salt
Dash of pepper
1/2 pound Velveeta
Pasteurized Process Cheese
Spread, cubed
1/3 cup chopped green pepper
1 3-ounce can sliced
mushrooms, drained
1/4 cup chopped onion
2 tablespoons chopped
pimiento
1 8-ounce package thin
spaghetti, cooked, drained
1/2 cup Kraft Grated
Parmesan Cheese
1 1/2 cups cooked ham strips

Heat oven 375°. Make white sauce with margarine, flour, milk and seasonings. Add Velveeta, green pepper, mushrooms, onion and pimiento; stir until Velveeta melts. Combine spaghetti and 1/4 cup Parmesan cheese; layer half of spaghetti, ham and Velveeta sauce in 12 x 8-inch baking dish; repeat layers. Top with remaining Parmesan cheese. Bake at 375°, 25 minutes. 6 to 8 servings.

Frank Whiz Macaroni

1 pound frankfurters
1 7-ounce package elbow
macaroni, cooked, drained
1 8-ounce jar Cheez Whiz
Pasteurized Process Cheese
Spread
¼ cup chopped green onion
1 tablespoon prepared
mustard

Simmer frankfurters in water 5 minutes; drain and slice diagonally. Combine frankfurters, macaroni, Cheez Whiz, onion and mustard. Heat. 4 to 6 servings.

Enchiladas El Paso

1 pound ground beef
2 cups (1-pound can) tomatoes
1 6-ounce can tomato paste
½ cup water
½ cup chopped onion
1 tablespoon chili powder
1¼ teaspoons salt
¼ teaspoon pepper
2 cups (8 ounces) shredded
Cracker Barrel Brand Sharp
Natural Cheddar Cheese
1 8-ounce package tortillas

Heat oven to 375°. Brown meat; drain. Stir in tomatoes, tomato paste, water, onion and seasonings. Simmer 10 minutes. Place rounded tablespoons of each, meat sauce and cheese, on each tortilla; roll up tightly. Place seam-side down in 12 x 8-inch baking dish; top with remaining sauce and cheese. Cover tightly with aluminum foil; bake at 375°, 25 minutes. 6 to 8 servings.

Nice to know: This dish may be made ahead, covered and refrigerated overnight. Bake, covered, at 375°, 50 minutes.

Lasagne

1 pound ground beef
½ cup chopped onion
1 6-ounce can tomato paste
1½ cups water
1 garlic clove, minced
2 teaspoons salt
¾ teaspoon oregano
¼ teaspoon pepper
8 ounces lasagne noodles,
cooked, drained
1 pound ricotta or cottage
cheese
2 6-ounce packages Kraft
Natural Low Moisture
Part-Skim Mozzarella Cheese
Slices
½ cup (2 ounces) Kraft Grated
Parmesan Cheese

Heat oven to 375°. Brown meat; drain. Add onion and cook until tender. Stir in tomato paste, water, garlic and seasonings; cover and simmer 30 minutes. In a 12 x 8-inch baking dish, layer half of noodles, meat sauce, ricotta cheese and Mozzarella cheese; repeat layers. Sprinkle with Parmesan cheese. Bake at 375°, 30 minutes. 6 to 8 servings.

Golden Meatball Casserole

1 pound ground beef
½ cup fresh bread crumbs
1 egg
1 teaspoon salt
All purpose oil
2 cups water
1 cup uncooked rice
2 large carrots, cut in quarters
½ cup chopped green pepper
¼ cup chopped onion
*½ pound Velveeta Pasteurized
Process Cheese Spread, cubed*

Combine meat, bread crumbs, egg and salt; mix lightly. Shape into 18 meatballs; brown in small amount of oil on all sides in large skillet. Drain. Add water, rice, carrots, green pepper and onion. Cover and simmer 25 minutes. Add Velveeta; heat until Velveeta melts. 4 to 6 servings.

El Rancho Casserole

1 pound ground beef
1 cup chopped onion
*1 7-ounce package
elbow macaroni*
*3½ cups (1-pound 12-ounce
can) tomatoes*
*1½ cups (12-ounce can) whole
kernel corn, undrained*
*½ pound Velveeta Pasteurized
Process Cheese Spread, cubed*
½ cup water
1 tablespoon chili powder
1 teaspoon salt
¼ teaspoon pepper

Brown meat; drain. Add onion and cook until tender. Stir in remaining ingredients. Cover and simmer, stirring occasionally, 30 to 35 minutes. 6 to 8 servings.

Plantation Supper

1 pound ground beef
½ cup chopped onion
1 cup milk
*1 8-ounce package Philadelphia
Brand Cream Cheese, cubed*
*1½ cups (1-pound can) whole
kernel corn, drained*
*4 cups (8 ounces) noodles,
cooked, drained*
¼ cup chopped pimiento
*1 3-ounce can sliced
mushrooms, drained*
1½ teaspoons salt
Dash of pepper

Brown meat; drain. Add onion; cook until tender. Stir in milk and cheese, mixing until well blended. Add remaining ingredients; heat. 8 servings.

Casserole Special

1 pound ground beef
½ cup chopped onion
1 8-ounce package Philadelphia
Brand Cream Cheese, cubed
1 can condensed cream of
mushroom soup
1½ cups (12-ounce can) whole
kernel corn, drained
1 2-ounce jar pimiento,
drained, chopped
1 teaspoon salt
Dash of pepper
1 can (9.5 ounces) refrigerated
buttermilk flaky biscuits

Heat oven to 375°. Brown meat; drain. Add onion; cook until tender. Stir in cheese and soup; mix well. Add corn, pimiento and seasonings; pour into 12 x 8-inch baking dish. Place biscuits around edge of baking dish; bake at 375°, 20 to 25 minutes. 6 servings.

Sicilian Supper

1 pound ground beef
½ cup chopped onion
1 6-ounce can tomato paste
¾ cup water
½ teaspoon salt
¼ teaspoon pepper
¾ cup milk
1 8-ounce package Philadelphia
Brand Cream Cheese, cubed
½ cup Kraft Grated
Parmesan Cheese
½ cup chopped green pepper
½ teaspoon garlic salt
2 cups noodles, cooked,
drained

Heat oven to 350°. Brown meat; drain. Add onion; cook until tender. Add tomato paste, water and seasonings; simmer 5 minutes. Heat milk and cream cheese over low heat, stirring until smooth. Stir in ¼ cup Parmesan cheese, green pepper, garlic salt and noodles. In 1½-quart casserole, layer half of noodle mixture and meat sauce; repeat layers. Bake at 350°, 20 minutes. Sprinkle with remaining Parmesan cheese. 6 servings.

South-of-the-Border Casserole

1 pound ground beef
½ cup chopped onion
2 8-ounce cans tomato sauce
1 tablespoon chili powder
1 teaspoon salt
12 tortillas (8-ounce package),
cut in half
2 cups (8 ounces) shredded
Cracker Barrel Brand Sharp
Natural Cheddar Cheese

Heat oven to 325°. Brown meat; drain. Add onion; cook until tender. Stir in tomato sauce and seasonings. Alternate layers of meat mixture, tortillas and cheese in 1½-quart casserole; bake at 325°, 20 minutes. 4 to 6 servings.

Potato Patch Casserole

1 pound ground beef
½ cup chopped onion
1 egg
¼ cup milk
¼ cup dry bread crumbs
1 teaspoon salt
¼ teaspoon pepper
¼ teaspoon celery salt
All purpose oil
*   *   *

2 tablespoons margarine
2 tablespoons flour
1 cup milk
1¼ teaspoons salt
Dash of pepper
*½ pound Velveeta Pasteurized
Process Cheese Spread, cubed*
4 cups sliced potatoes
*1 10-ounce package frozen
peas and carrots, thawed*

Heat oven to 350°. Combine meat, onion, egg, milk, bread crumbs and seasonings; mix lightly. Shape into 10 meatballs; brown in oil. Make white sauce with margarine, flour, milk and seasonings. Add Velveeta; stir until melted. Combine potatoes and peas and carrots; place in 12 x 8-inch baking dish. Arrange meatballs around edge of dish; cover with Velveeta sauce. Cover dish with aluminum foil; bake at 350°, 1 hour. Uncover; continue baking 30 minutes. 4 to 6 servings.

Mostaccioli

½ pound ground beef
½ cup chopped green pepper
½ cup chopped onion
2 cups (1-pound can) tomatoes
1 6-ounce can tomato paste
½ cup water
1 bay leaf
½ teaspoon salt
¼ teaspoon pepper
*8 ounces mostaccioli noodles,
cooked, drained*
*½ pound Velveeta Pasteurized
Process Cheese Spread,
thinly sliced*
Kraft Grated Parmesan Cheese

Heat oven to 350°. Brown meat; add green pepper and onion. Cook until tender. Stir in tomatoes, tomato paste, water and seasonings. In a 2-quart casserole, layer half the noodles, meat sauce and Velveeta; repeat layers. Sprinkle with Parmesan cheese. Bake at 350°, 30 minutes. 6 to 8 servings.

Opposite: Mostaccioli

FAIR Tuna 'Tater Puff

1/4 *pound Velveeta Pasteurized*
Process Cheese Spread, cubed
2 *cups hot mashed potatoes*
1 *egg, beaten*
1/2 *cup chopped celery*
1/3 *cup chopped onion*
2 *tablespoons margarine*
1/4 *cup chopped pimiento*
Dash of pepper
1 *7-ounce can tuna, drained,*
flaked

Heat oven to 350°. Combine Velveeta and potatoes; add egg. Cook celery and onion in margarine until tender; add to potatoes. Stir in remaining ingredients; pour into 1-quart casserole. Bake at 350°, 40 to 45 minutes. 6 servings.

Country Casserole

1 1/2 *cups milk*
1 *8-ounce package Philadelphia*
Brand Cream Cheese, cubed
1/4 *cup (1 ounce) Kraft Grated*
Parmesan Cheese
1/2 *teaspoon onion salt*
1/4 *teaspoon oregano, crumbled*
1 *7-ounce package spaghetti,*
cooked, drained
1 *10-ounce package frozen*
peas, cooked, drained
1 *7-ounce can tuna, drained,*
flaked
1 *3-ounce can sliced*
mushrooms, drained
1 *tablespoon chopped*
pimiento
1 *tablespoon chopped onion*

Heat oven to 350°. Heat milk and cream cheese over low heat, stirring until smooth. Add Parmesan cheese, onion salt and oregano; mix well. Add remaining ingredients; mix. Place in 2-quart casserole; cover and bake at 350°, 20 minutes. 6 to 8 servings.

Tempting Tuna Bake

2 *tablespoons margarine*
2 *tablespoons flour*
1 1/2 *cups milk*
1/4 *teaspoon salt*
Dash of pepper
1 1/2 *cups (6 ounces) shredded*
Cracker Barrel Brand Sharp
Natural Cheddar Cheese
4 *ounces spaghetti,*
cooked, drained
2 *7-ounce cans tuna,*
drained, flaked
1/3 *cup sliced ripe olives*
1/3 *cup chopped onion*
1/4 *cup slivered almonds,*
toasted

Heat oven to 350°. Make white sauce with margarine, flour, milk and seasonings. Add 1 cup cheese; stir until melted. Stir in spaghetti, tuna, olives, onion and nuts. Pour into 1 1/2-quart casserole; bake at 350°, 25 minutes. Sprinkle with remaining cheese; return to oven until cheese melts. 6 to 8 servings.
Nice to know: This dish may be made ahead, covered and refrigerated overnight. Remove cover and bake at 350°, 55 minutes.

Old-Fashioned Macaroni and Cheese

¼ cup margarine
¼ cup flour
2 cups milk
1 teaspoon salt
2 cups (8 ounces) shredded Cracker Barrel Brand Sharp Natural Cheddar Cheese
1 7-ounce package elbow macaroni, cooked, drained

Heat oven to 350°. Make white sauce with margarine, flour, milk and salt; add cheese, reserving ½ cup; stir until melted. Layer half of macaroni and cheese sauce in 1½-quart casserole; repeat layers. Top with remaining cheese. Bake at 350°, 20 to 25 minutes. 6 to 8 servings.

Calico Macaroni

¼ cup chopped carrots
¼ cup chopped onion
¼ cup chopped green pepper
2 tablespoons margarine
1 7-ounce package elbow macaroni, cooked, drained
1 8-ounce jar Cheez Whiz Pasteurized Process Cheese Spread

Cook carrots, onion and green pepper in margarine until tender. Combine vegetables, macaroni and Cheese Whiz; stir until well blended. Heat. 4 to 6 servings.

Macaroni Tomato Bake

1 7-ounce package elbow macaroni, cooked, drained
1¾ cups milk
¾ cup (3 ounces) Kraft Grated Parmesan Cheese
⅓ cup chopped onion
3 eggs, beaten
1½ teaspoons salt
¼ teaspoon pepper
1 6-ounce package Kraft Natural Low Moisture Part-Skim Mozzarella Cheese Slices, cut in thin strips
2 tomatoes
1½ cups fresh bread crumbs
2 tablespoons margarine, melted

Heat oven to 350°. Combine macaroni, milk, ½ cup Parmesan cheese, onion, eggs, seasonings and Mozzarella cheese. Pour half of macaroni mixture into 2-quart casserole. Top with 1 tomato, sliced. Add remaining macaroni mixture. Toss crumbs in margarine and sprinkle on top. Cut remaining tomato in wedges; arrange on casserole. Bake at 350°, 45 minutes. Sprinkle with remaining Parmesan cheese; return to oven for 5 minutes. 8 servings.

Great Cheese Pies

Who's for pizza? Everybody from six to sixty. Who's for
quiche? The family, the guests—everyone who tries
a slice of any one of these imaginative cheese pies will
become converted on the spot to the pie-from-cheese clan.

Pizza Napoli

1 package dry yeast
1⅓ cups lukewarm water
2 tablespoons all purpose oil
3½ cups flour
1 teaspoon salt
1 8-ounce can tomato sauce
1 6-ounce can tomato paste
½ cup water
1 teaspoon oregano, crumbled
¼ teaspoon salt
1 10-ounce package frozen
asparagus spears, thawed
1½ cups sliced pitted ripe olives
2 8-ounce packages Kraft
Shredded Natural Low
Moisture Part-Skim
Mozzarella Cheese

Dissolve yeast in water; add oil. Combine flour and salt; add yeast mixture. Mix until well blended. On a floured surface, knead dough until smooth, about 10 minutes. Place dough in a greased bowl. Cover; let rise in a warm place until double in bulk, about 2 hours. Punch down; divide dough in half. Roll each half to fit a lightly greased 14-inch pizza pan. Heat oven to 425°. Combine tomato sauce, tomato paste, water, oregano and salt; mix well. Spread half of mixture over each pizza crust. Top each pizza with half of asparagus and olives; sprinkle each pizza with half of cheese. Bake at 425°, 20 minutes. 12 servings.

Another way: Omit asparagus and olives. Top each pizza with 1 medium green pepper cut in thin strips and 1 cup frozen French-fried onion rings before sprinkling with cheese.

Pizza Milano

1¾ cups flour
1 teaspoon baking powder
1 teaspoon salt
⅔ cup milk
¼ cup all purpose oil
1 8-ounce can tomato sauce
½ teaspoon oregano, crumbled
Dash of salt
½ pound pepperoni, sliced
1 8-ounce package Kraft
Shredded Natural Low
Moisture Part-Skim
Mozzarella Cheese

Heat oven to 425°. Combine flour, baking powder and salt; add milk and oil. Stir with a fork until mixture forms a ball. Knead about 10 times on an unfloured surface. Roll dough to fit a 14-inch pizza pan. Combine tomato sauce, oregano and salt; mix well. Spread over pizza crust; top with pepperoni. Sprinkle with cheese; bake at 425°, 15 to 20 minutes. 6 to 8 servings.

Another way: Omit pepperoni. Top pizza with one 3-ounce jar sliced mushrooms, drained, and 2 small zucchini, sliced, before sprinkling with cheese.

Cheddar Cheese Pie

2 cups (8 ounces) shredded
Cracker Barrel Brand Sharp
Natural Cheddar Cheese
2 tablespoons flour
4 eggs, slightly beaten
1½ cups milk
¾ cup diced cooked ham
¼ teaspoon salt
Dash of pepper
1 9-inch unbaked pastry shell

Heat oven to 350°. Toss cheese with flour. Add eggs, milk, ham and seasonings; mix well. Pour into pastry shell; bake at 350°, 1 hour. 6 servings.

Ski Trail Cheese Pie

2 cups (8 ounces) shredded
Cracker Barrel Brand Sharp
Natural Cheddar Cheese
2 tablespoons flour
½ teaspoon salt
¼ teaspoon dry mustard
8 slices crisply cooked
bacon, crumbled
4 eggs, beaten
1 8-ounce can tomato sauce
½ cup milk
¼ cup chopped onion
1 9-inch unbaked pastry shell

Heat oven to 350°. Toss cheese with flour and seasonings. Combine bacon, eggs, tomato sauce, milk and onion, mixing until well blended. Add cheese mixture; mix well. Pour into pastry shell; bake at 350°, 40 to 45 minutes. 6 servings.

Florentine Swiss Pie

2 cups (8 ounces) shredded
Kraft Aged Natural
Swiss Cheese
2 tablespoons flour
1¼ cups milk
3 eggs, beaten
½ teaspoon salt
Dash of nutmeg
Dash of pepper
1 9-inch unbaked pastry shell
1 3-ounce can sliced
mushrooms, drained
1 medium zucchini, sliced
3 large pitted ripe olives,
sliced
¼ pound pepperoni, sliced

Heat oven to 350°. Toss 1½ cups cheese with flour. Combine milk, eggs and seasonings. Stir in cheese mixture. Pour into pastry shell. Bake at 350°, 35 to 40 minutes. Arrange mushrooms, zucchini, olives and pepperoni in concentric rings on pie; sprinkle with remaining cheese. Return to oven; continue baking 20 minutes. 6 to 8 servings.

Swiss-Spinach Quiche

1 can (4.5 ounces) refrigerated
buttermilk biscuits
1 8-ounce package Kraft
Natural Swiss Cheese Slices,
cut in thin strips
2 tablespoons flour
1 cup milk
3 eggs, beaten
½ teaspoon salt
Dash of pepper
Dash of nutmeg
1 10-ounce package frozen
chopped spinach, cooked,
drained

Heat oven to 350°. Place biscuits in ungreased 9-inch
quiche pan (or 9-inch pie pan),
pressing pieces together to
form a crust. Toss cheese with
flour. Combine milk, eggs and
seasonings. Add cheese mixture and spinach; mix well.
Pour into crust. Bake at 350°,
1 hour. 8 servings.

Cheddar Pasties

1 package pie crust mix
(2 9-inch crusts)
1½ cups (6 ounces) Cracker
Barrel Brand Sharp Natural
Cheddar Cheese
2 cups cubed beef or pork
1 tablespoon margarine
1 cup boiling water
1 cup cooked potatoes
1 cup sliced onions
1 teaspoon salt
Dash of pepper

Heat oven to 375°. Combine
pie crust mix and cheese. Prepare pie crust mix as directed
on package. Divide dough in
16 portions; roll each to 5-inch
circle. Brown meat in margarine. Pour water over vegetables. Simmer 10 minutes; drain.
Toss together meat and vegetables; add salt and pepper.
Place 2 tablespoons of meat
mixture on each pastry circle;
fold over and press edges together to seal. Place on baking
sheet. Bake at 375°, 20 minutes.
8 servings.

"Philly" Quiche au Jambon

1 10-inch unbaked pastry shell
1 cup milk
1 8-ounce package Philadelphia
Brand Cream Cheese, cubed
¼ cup chopped onion
1 tablespoon margarine
4 eggs, beaten
1 cup finely chopped ham
¼ cup chopped pimiento
¼ teaspoon dill weed
Dash of pepper

Bake pastry shell at 400°, 12 to
15 minutes; cool. Reduce temperature to 350°. Heat milk
over low heat; add cream
cheese, stirring until melted.
Cook onion in margarine until
tender. Gradually add cheese
sauce to · eggs; stir in onion,
ham, pimiento and seasonings.
Pour into pastry shell; bake at
350°, 35 to 40 minutes. 8 servings.

Alpine Appetizers

6 slices bacon
½ cup chopped onion
⅓ cup chopped green pepper
3 eggs, slightly beaten
1 cup half and half
½ teaspoon salt
Dash of Tabasco sauce
*1 cup (4 ounces) shredded Kraft
Aged Natural Swiss Cheese*
1 9-inch unbaked pastry shell

Heat oven to 350°. Cook bacon until crisp; drain, reserving 2 tablespoons bacon fat. Cook onion and green pepper in bacon fat until tender. Combine eggs, half and half and seasonings; mix well. Add cheese, onion and green pepper. Pour into pastry shell; crumble bacon and sprinkle over top. Bake at 350°, 40 to 45 minutes. 16 appetizers.

Quiche Bretagne

½ cup mayonnaise
½ teaspoon salt
2 eggs, beaten
¼ cup milk
2 tablespoons white wine
*1 8-ounce package Kraft
Natural Swiss Cheese Slices,
chopped*
2 tablespoons flour
*1½ cups (6½-ounce can)
crabmeat, drained, flaked*
⅓ cup sliced celery
¼ cup sliced green onion
1 9-inch unbaked pastry shell

Heat oven to 350°. Combine mayonnaise, salt, eggs, milk and wine; mix until well blended. Toss cheese with flour. Add cheese mixture, crabmeat, celery and onion to mayonnaise mixture; mix well. Pour into pastry shell. Bake at 350°, 45 minutes. 6 to 8 servings.
Another way: Omit crabmeat. Add 1 cup chopped cooked shrimp.

Quiche Lorraine

1½ cups half and half
4 eggs, slightly beaten
½ teaspoon salt
Dash of pepper
*2 cups (8 ounces) shredded
Kraft Aged Natural Swiss
Cheese*
2 tablespoons flour
*8 slices crisply cooked
bacon, crumbled*
1 9-inch unbaked pastry shell

Heat oven to 350°. Combine half and half, eggs and seasonings; mix well. Toss cheese with flour; add cheese mixture and bacon to egg mixture. Pour into pastry shell; bake at 350°, 40 to 45 minutes. 6 servings.
Another way: Substitute ¾ cup chopped cooked ham for bacon.

Opposite: Quiche Lorraine

Potato-topped Pie

1½ pounds ground beef
2 cups (8 ounces) shredded
Cracker Barrel Brand Sharp
Natural Cheddar Cheese
1 egg
⅓ cup catsup
¼ cup dry bread crumbs
¼ cup chopped onion
¼ cup chopped green pepper
1 teaspoon salt
Dash of pepper
2 cups hot mashed potatoes

Heat oven to 350°. Combine meat, 1½ cups cheese, egg, catsup, bread crumbs, onion, green pepper, salt and pepper; mix lightly. Pat into 9-inch pie plate. Bake at 350°, 30 minutes; drain off excess fat. Spread potatoes evenly over meat. Sprinkle remaining cheese over top. Return to oven until cheese begins to melt. 6 to 8 servings.

Manchester Sausage Pie

1 package pie crust mix
(2 9-inch crusts)
1 pound pork sausage
⅓ cup chopped green onion
3 tablespoons margarine
3 tablespoons flour
1 cup milk
1½ cups (6-ounces) shredded
Cracker Barrel Brand Sharp
Natural Cheddar Cheese
2 teaspoons prepared
horseradish

Heat oven to 375°. Prepare pie crust as directed on package. Divide dough in 2 portions; roll each to 11-inch circle. Line 9-inch pie plate with pastry. Brown sausage. Add onion and cook until tender; drain. Make white sauce with margarine, flour and milk. Add cheese; cook, stirring constantly, until cheese is melted. Combine meat mixture, sauce and horseradish; mix well. Pour meat mixture into pastry-lined pie plate; cover with top crust. Flute edges and slit top. Bake at 375°, 35 minutes. Let stand 10 minutes before serving. 6 to 8 servings.

Chicken Little's Pot Pies

1 cup boiling water
1 cup cubed potatoes
½ cup sliced carrots
½ cup sliced celery
¼ cup chopped onion
2 tablespoons margarine
2 tablespoons flour
1 teaspoon salt
1 cup milk
2 cups (8 ounces) shredded
Cracker Barrel Brand Sharp
Natural Cheddar Cheese
2 cups diced cooked chicken
½ package pie crust mix
(1 9-inch crust)

Heat oven to 425°. Pour water over vegetables. Simmer 10 minutes; drain. Make white sauce with margarine, flour, salt and milk. Add cheese; cook, stirring constantly, until cheese is melted. Stir in vegetables and chicken. Spoon chicken mixture into 4 5½-inch pie plates. Prepare pie crust as directed on package. Divide dough in 4 portions; roll each to 7-inch circle. Fit each dish with crust. Flute and slit crust. Bake at 425°, 30 minutes. 4 servings.

Meat Pie Roma

1 pound ground beef
½ cup chopped green pepper
⅓ cup chopped onion
1 6-ounce can tomato paste
¾ cup water
1 teaspoon salt
½ teaspoon oregano
¼ teaspoon garlic powder
Dash of pepper
1 8-ounce package refrigerated flaky biscuits
⅓ cup (1½-ounces) Kraft Grated Parmesan Cheese
1 6-ounce package Kraft Natural Low Moisture Part-Skim Mozzarella Cheese Slices

Heat oven to 400°. Brown meat; drain. Add green pepper, onion, tomato paste, water and seasonings; simmer 10 minutes. Line greased 9-inch pie plate with biscuits; sprinkle with ¼ cup Parmesan cheese. Fill with ½ of meat mixture and 2 slices of Mozzarella cheese. Top with remaining meat and Parmesan cheese. Bake at 400°, 15 to 20 minutes. Cut remaining Moz-

zarella cheese into strips; place on top of meat pie to form lattice. Return to oven until cheese melts. 6 to 8 servings.

Crostate con Formaggio

½ cup (2 ounces) Kraft Grated Parmesan Cheese
1 package pie crust mix (2 9-inch crusts)
⅓ cup chopped onion
⅓ cup chopped green pepper
1½ cups sliced zucchini
1 garlic clove, minced
2 tablespoons margarine
1 1-pound can whole peeled tomatoes, crushed
1 3-ounce can mushrooms, drained
½ teaspoon salt
¼ teaspoon oregano
Dash of pepper

Heat oven to 375°. Add ⅓ cup cheese to pie crust mix. Prepare pie crust as directed on package. Divide dough in 8 portions; roll each to 7-inch circle. Line 8 4-inch tart pans; flute edge. Cook onion, green pepper, zucchini and garlic in margarine until tender; drain. Add tomatoes, mushrooms and seasonings; simmer 10 minutes. Fill each tart shell with ⅓ cup of vegetable mixture; top with remaining cheese. Bake at 375°, 25 minutes. 8 tarts.

Sauces, Rabbits and Other Savories

Cheese sauces to pour on, cheese sauces to spoon on, cheese sauces to serve over—every one of them an experience in good eating; you'll see blissful smiles on faces all around when you serve these fine-flavor treats to family or guests.

Cheddar Cheese Sauce

2 tablespoons margarine
2 tablespoons flour
¼ teaspoon salt
Dash of cayenne
Dash of dry mustard
1 cup milk
1 cup (4 ounces) shredded
Cracker Barrel Brand Sharp
Natural Cheddar Cheese

Melt margarine in saucepan over low heat. Blend in flour and seasonings. Add milk; cook, stirring constantly, until thickened. Add cheese, stirring until melted. 1⅓ cups.

"Philly" Chive Sauce

¾ cup milk
1 8-ounce package Philadelphia
Brand Cream Cheese, cubed
1 tablespoon chopped chives
1 teaspoon lemon juice
¼ teaspoon garlic salt

Heat milk in saucepan over low heat. Add cream cheese, stirring until melted. Blend in remaining ingredients. Serve over hot cooked potatoes, green beans, broccoli or asparagus. 1⅓ cups.

Velveeta Sauce

½ pound Velveeta Pasteurized
Process Cheese Spread, cubed
¼ cup milk

Heat Velveeta and milk over low heat; stir until sauce is smooth. 1 cup.

Delmonico Sauce

½ cup milk
1 8-ounce package Philadelphia
Brand Cream Cheese, cubed
¼ cup (2 ounces) Kraft Cold
Pack Blue Cheese, crumbled
Dash of onion salt

Heat milk and cream cheese in saucepan over low heat, stirring until smooth. Blend in remaining ingredients. Serve over hot vegetables. Top with additional Blue cheese, if desired. 3 to 4 servings.

Mornay Sauce

¼ cup margarine
¼ cup flour
2 cups milk
½ teaspoon salt
Dash of pepper
1 cup (4 ounces) shredded
Kraft Aged Natural Swiss
Cheese
¼ cup Kraft Grated
Parmesan Cheese

Make white sauce with margarine, flour, milk and seasonings. Add Swiss cheese and Parmesan cheese; stir until melted. Serve over hot cooked broccoli, asparagus, sliced turkey or ham. 2¾ cups.
Nice to know: This sauce can be reheated.

"Philly" Orange Sauce

1 8-ounce package Philadelphia
    Brand Cream Cheese
¼ cup orange juice
2 tablespoons sugar
1 teaspoon grated orange rind

Combine softened cream cheese and remaining ingredients, mixing until well blended. Chill. Serve over fruit, pound cake or angel food cake. 1¼ cups.

"Philly" Dessert Sauce

1 8-ounce package Philadelphia
    Brand Cream Cheese
¼ cup sugar
2 eggs, separated
1½ teaspoons vanilla

Combine softened cream cheese, sugar, egg yolks and vanilla, mixing until well blended. Fold in stiffly beaten egg whites. 2 cups.
Nice to know: This sauce is excellent for serving over gingerbread, upside-down cake or baked puddings.

Epicurean "Philly" Sauce

1 8-ounce package Philadelphia
    Brand Cream Cheese, cubed
¼ cup milk
2 tablespoons margarine
¼ cup dry white wine
2 tablespoons chopped parsley
2 tablespoons finely chopped
    onion
¼ teaspoon salt
Dash of pepper

Heat cream cheese, milk and margarine over low heat; stir until smooth. Stir in remaining ingredients; heat. Serve over meat or fish. 1½ cups.

Hot Horseradish Sauce

1 8-ounce package Philadelphia
    Brand Cream Cheese, cubed
⅓ cup milk
2 tablespoons prepared
    horseradish
¼ teaspoon salt
Dash of cayenne

Heat cream cheese and milk in saucepan over low heat, stirring until smooth. Blend in remaining ingredients. Serve over ham, beef or hot cooked vegetables. 1⅓ cups.

Parisian Wine Sauce

1 8-ounce package Philadelphia
Brand Cream Cheese
⅓ cup milk
2 tablespoons dry white wine
1 tablespoon chopped green
onion
¼ teaspoon salt
Dash of cayenne

Heat cream cheese and milk in saucepan over low heat, stirring until smooth. Blend in remaining ingredients. Serve over fish, chicken or pork. 1⅓ cups.

Perky Cheese Sauce

½ cup mayonnaise
1 4-ounce container Kraft
Whipped Cream Cheese with
Bacon and Horseradish
2 teaspoons chopped green
onion

Gradually add mayonnaise to whipped cream cheese; mix well. Stir in onion. Serve over cold roast beef. 1 cup.

Dilly Cheese Sauce

½ pound Velveeta Pasteurized
Process Cheese Spread,
cubed
½ cup salad dressing
¼ cup milk
¼ teaspoon dill weed

Heat Velveeta, salad dressing and milk over low heat until sauce is smooth, stirring constantly. Add dill. 1½ cups.

Sauce Louis

1 8-ounce package Philadelphia
Brand Cream Cheese, cubed
¼ cup milk
½ cup chili sauce
½ teaspoon Worcestershire
sauce
¼ teaspoon prepared
horseradish
¼ teaspoon salt
Dash of cayenne

Heat cream cheese and milk in saucepan over low heat, stirring until smooth. Blend in remaining ingredients; chill. Serve over shrimp, cold vegetables or hard-cooked eggs. 1½ cups.

"Philly" Bearnaise Sauce

2 tablespoons chopped green
onions
1 teaspoon tarragon, crushed
3 tablespoons vinegar
1 8-ounce package Philadelphia
Brand Cream Cheese, cubed
⅓ cup milk
1 tablespoon lime juice
1 tablespoon chopped chives

Boil onion and tarragon in vinegar until vinegar is evaporated. Add remaining ingredients. Cook over low heat until sauce is smooth, stirring constantly. Serve over beef, fish or eggs. 1 cup.

77

Classic Cheese Rabbit

2 cups (8 ounces) shredded
Cracker Barrel Brand Sharp
Natural Cheddar Cheese
½ cup beer or ale
2 tablespoons margarine
½ teaspoon paprika
¼ teaspoon dry mustard
1 egg, slightly beaten
White bread, toasted, cut
in triangles

Heat cheese, beer, margarine
and seasonings in double boiler; stir until sauce is smooth.
Blend in egg; stir until thickened. Serve over toast. 4 servings.
Other ways: Stir in 6 slices
crisply cooked bacon, crumbled; top with French-fried
onions; top with hard-cooked
egg slices; serve over shoestring potatoes.

Country Rabbit

1 8-ounce jar Cheez Whiz
Pasteurized Process Cheese
Spread
½ cup mayonnaise
1 cup chopped cooked chicken
1 tablespoon chopped green
onion
1 tablespoon chopped pimiento
White bread, toasted, cut in
triangles

Combine Cheez Whiz and
mayonnaise in saucepan. Add
chicken, onion and pimiento.
Heat; serve over toast. 3 to 4
servings.

Spanish Rabbit

¼ cup chopped onion
¼ cup chopped green pepper
¼ cup margarine
¼ cup flour
1¾ cups milk
1 teaspoon salt
¼ teaspoon pepper
1 cup (4 ounces) shredded
Cracker Barrel Brand Sharp
Natural Cheddar Cheese
1 cup chopped peeled tomato
1½ cups (6½-ounce can)
crabmeat, drained, flaked
8 slices white bread, toasted,
cut in triangles

Cook onion and green pepper
in margarine; blend in flour.
Gradually add milk, stirring
until thickened. Add seasonings and cheese; stir until
melted. Stir in tomato and crabmeat; heat. Serve over toast. 8
servings.

Shrimp Rabbit

½ cup chopped green pepper
2 tablespoons chopped onion
2 tablespoons margarine
1½ cups cooked shrimp
½ pound Velveeta Pasteurized
Process Cheese Spread, cubed
⅔ cup milk
4 slices white bread, toasted,
cut in triangles

Cook green pepper and onion in
margarine until tender. Add
shrimp; heat. Heat Velveeta
and milk over low heat; stir until sauce is smooth. Add shrimp
and vegetables; mix. Serve over
toast. 4 servings.

Opposite: Classic Cheese Rabbit

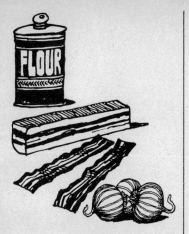

Creole Rabbit

4 slices bacon
½ cup finely chopped onion
½ cup chopped green pepper
¼ cup flour
1 cup milk
1 medium tomato, peeled, chopped
1 cup (4 ounces) shredded Cracker Barrel Brand Sharp Natural Cheddar Cheese
1 teaspoon Worcestershire sauce
½ teaspoon salt
White bread, toasted, cut in triangles

Cook bacon until crisp. Remove from skillet; crumble. Cook onion and green pepper in bacon fat until tender; blend in flour. Stir in milk and tomato; cook until thickened. Add bacon, cheese, Worcestershire sauce and salt; stir until cheese is melted. Serve over toast. 6 servings.

Welshman's Rabbit

2 tablespoons margarine
2 tablespoons flour
1 cup milk
¼ teaspoon dry mustard
Dash of cayenne
2 cups (8 ounces) shredded Cracker Barrel Brand Sharp Natural Cheddar Cheese
White bread, toasted, cut in triangles

Make white sauce with margarine, flour, milk and seasonings. Add cheese; stir until melted. Serve over toast; sprinkle with paprika, if desired. 6 servings.

Gold Coast Rabbit

2 cups (8 ounces) shredded Cracker Barrel Brand Sharp Natural Cheddar Cheese
½ cup milk
2 tablespoons margarine
½ teaspoon paprika
1 egg, slightly beaten
1 4½-ounce can shrimp, drained
4 hard-cooked eggs, quartered
White bread, toasted, cut in triangles

Heat cheese, milk, margarine and paprika over low heat; stir until smooth. Blend in egg; stir until thickened. Add shrimp. Arrange eggs on toast; top with sauce. 4 servings.

The Romance of Cheese

Where did cheese originate? How is it made? How many kinds of cheese are there? How should cheese be stored? Can it be frozen? These and dozens of other questions about one of the world's favorite —and most nutritious—foods are answered here.

Cheese-making has a long history, its origins lost in the far reaches of time. The discovery of cheese was probably an accident—as simple an accident as someone's tasting curdled milk and finding the taste to his liking. Two legends persist and are worth repeating because they are, like so many legends, both interesting and likely stories.

A News-Making Camel Ride

The first legend concerns a long-ago desert tribesman who set out on a journey with a container of milk—probably mare's or camel's milk—in that day's ordinary milk container, the dried stomach of a sheep. In the broiling desert sun he mounted his camel and took off on a ride as bumpy and lurchy in those days as a camel ride remains to this day.

When he stopped to refresh himself, he found the milk separated into a thin, watery substance (whey) and a thickened mass (curds)—a result of the warmth of the day and the churning motion of the ride he had taken, helped along by the action of the rennet, an enzyme, in the sheep's stomach. He tasted the mass of curds and was delighted. We can imagine that he could hardly wait to get home to share his great discovery with his family and friends.

A Shepherd's Forgotten Lunch

The second legend goes like this: Long, long ago a herdsman went out to tend his sheep, taking with him a lunch of fresh ewe's or goat's milk cheese and a chunk of bread. He laid his lunch aside—perhaps in the shade of a tree, perhaps in a cave to keep the food cool—and went about his business. Something kept him from his lunch that day and for several days thereafter. When he finally did get back to it, he found the cheese in a condition that he probably thought of as "spoiled." It was veined with blue mold. Gingerly he tasted the cheese and, to his surprise, found that it was delicious.

Cheese in Recorded History

However cheese came to be discovered, it has been a staple—and nutritious and tasty—food of many peoples for many years. The Sumarians of 4000 B.C. ate cheese, as tablets dating back to that time testify. Archaeologists have similarly established that long-ago Egyptians and Chaldeans knew what a wonderful food could be made from clabbered milk. The ancient Greeks thought it a fit offering to their gods. David, on his way to deliver cheese to Saul's camp, interrupted his journey to fight the giant, Goliath.

Among the many things of which Homer sang, cheese was one. The Greeks trained their athletes on cheese and made their wedding cakes of it. The Romans knew a number of kinds of cheese. Returning from his journeys, Marco Polo told of, among other wonders, the many varieties of cheese, and the secrets of making it, that he had encountered.

Armies, so the old saying goes, travel on their stomachs, and the men of many an ancient army, including those of Julius Caesar and Genghis Khan, carried cheese to sustain them. Visitors to ancient Sicily brought home tales of incredibly delicious cheesecakes. Charlemagne, it is said, had a great fondness for Roquefort.

Indeed, a history of cheese might be said to be a capsule history of the world.

Dutch Cheese, Dutch Thrift

An old story told to demonstrate Dutch thrift and industry says that for centuries women all over Europe sat in their kitchens with their feet and hands busy with rocking cradles, knitting, spinning, preparing food for cooking—but only in Holland was there, as well, under the seat cushion of each chair, a wheel of cheese ripening.

Where Did That Word Come From?

How did we come by the word *cheese*? The ancient Greeks drained their cheese in wicker baskets called *formos*. The word became *forma* in Latin, and from that root came today's Italian *formaggio* and French *fromage*. The Latin word for cheese itself was *caseus*, and from that root sprang the German *Käse*, Dutch *kaas*, Gaelic *câis*, Welsh *caws*, Portuguese *queijo* and Spanish *queso*. The same root produced the Old English word *cese* and a variation, *cyse*, which evolved into our present-day *cheese*.

Whatever it is called, in whatever country, there are by now a very great many varieties of cheese in existence—estimates range from 700 to 2,000. France alone claims 500. Some 200 kinds are made in the United States.

Cheese is hearty, nourishing fare. Bread and cheese—sometimes with a handful of olives or a fresh fig or two or some apricots from a nearby tree—along with a beaker of the sour local wine has fed many a peasant in many a land. But cheese has snob appeal, too. Gourmets speak of fine cheeses in hushed tones: Crottin de Chavignol, for example, a small, medium-firm salted goat's milk cheese from the Berry district of France that sells in Paris markets, during its short season, at the equivalent of three dollars a pound.

Many cheeses are named after the places in which they are made—or were first made. Cheddar is the name of a village near Bristol, England, where its name-sake cheese first saw light; today the town is still the center of a thriving cheese industry. Limburger is named after Limburg, Belgium.

Curds and Whey

Cheese-making may have begun as a happy accident, but it has grown into a huge industry whose production is based on scientific principles and surrounded by strict regulations to control flavor, wholesomeness, uniformity and purity. Nevertheless, it all begins now, as then, with the separation of milk into curds and whey.

The kind of milk—sheep, buffalo, reindeer, cow or goat—begins the determination of the taste and texture of the finished cheese. By variations in preparation of curds, by the addition of such friendly organisms as bacteria and mold and by the conditions of the curing or ripening, the differences among the many kinds of cheese are caused.

Reduced to its simplest definition, natural cheese is the solid or casein portion of milk (curds) separated from the whey. Coagulation is facilitated and controlled by the action of rennet or of lactic acid or both. Here are the basic steps in the manufacture of natural cheese.

1. PREPARING THE MILK

Fresh milk is received at the cheese factory from farms. It is scientifically tested and heat treated; fat content is adjusted; the milk is then pumped into vats.

2. ADDING COLORING, STARTER AND RENNET

Coloring is not used in all cheeses, but for a

golden-colored cheese, for example, a vegetable coloring is added to the milk. Then the starter, a pure culture of microorganisms, is added to help firm up the curd particles and develop individual characteristics of the cheese variety being manufactured. Rennet extract, containing the enzyme, coagulates the milk into a custard-like mass, which is called *curd*.

3. CUTTING THE CURD AND COOKING

After the curd reaches the firmness of custard, it is cut into small cubes to permit the watery whey to begin to separate. Curds and whey are then heated to the required cooking temperature for the kind of cheese being made—this firms the curd and hastens the separation of the whey from the curd.

4. DRAINING THE WHEY

The whey is removed from the curd by simple drainage or by one of several mechanical methods.

5. SALTING THE CURD

The time that salt is added, and the amount, has a definite effect on the type of cheese produced. Sometimes salt is added after pressing (step 6).

6. PRESSING AND CURING THE CHEESE

The salted curd is weighed and pressed into forms to produce a solid block of cheese. The cheese is then kept in temperature-controlled storage rooms to cure until the desired texture and flavor develop.

Family Cheese Groups

Each cheese, of the cured cheese varieties, has its own specific range of time and temperature, its own particular conditions of curing which, taken together, result in the development of that cheese. Depending on the sharpness desired, cheeses are aged up to twelve months, some up to twenty-four months. The cheese is then cut in portions of convenient size and packaged in sealed wrappings to suit popular demand.

Just as there are many nations in the world, there are great families—related groups—of cheese. All varieties stem from nine basic families: Cheddar, Dutch, provolone, Swiss, blue, Parmesan, fresh, surface-ripened and whey. Most of these cheeses originated in the Old World; those we find at supermarkets today may be imported or may be manufactured in this country.

Cheddar Cheese Family

Cheddar is the most popular cheese in the United States. Like all other varieties of natural cheese, it is made according to the six basic steps. The variation that sets Cheddar apart occurs in step 4. At this point the curd is allowed to knit together and is turned and piled to expel the whey. This procedure—known as cheddaring—develops the characteristic body and texture. The flattened slab is then "milled"—cut into smaller pieces—and placed in a hoop or mold.

Colby is another member of the Cheddar family. In making it, the curd particles are stirred and not allowed to knit together, resulting in a more open-textured cheese. The drained curd is washed with cool water, which gives a cheese a higher moisture content and milder flavor.

Monterey or Monterey Jack cheese was developed by monks in southern California in the early days of California history. This creamy white cheese is similar to Colby, although it has a higher moisture content, a softer consistency, and a more open texture.

The Dutch Cheeses

The most popular varieties of cheese from Holland are Edam and Gouda. Both are semisoft to hard, and both are sweet-curd cheeses made from cows' milk. Both have a characteristic milky, nut-like flavor that varies in intensity with the age of the cheese.

In the United States Edam is the familiar red cannonball-shaped cheese, usually weighing from ¾ pound to 4½ pounds. In Holland, Edam is often found in the natural gold color, without the waxy red covering.

Gouda comes in one of two shapes: a flattened sphere or a rectangular loaf. A Gouda may weigh from six to fifty pounds, but probably the most familiar is the "baby Gouda," weighing a pound or less—the size most often seen in our supermarkets. Gouda, too, may or may not have a red wax coating.

Special metal or hardwood molds lined with cheesecloth are used in the "pressing" step of the manufacture of Edam and Gouda. These molds, which give the cheeses their characteristic shape, consist of a round lower section perforated for draining and a round cover.

Cheeses made by this same method may include mixtures of cumin, caraway and other spices. Some examples are noekkelost, Leyden and cuminost.

The Provolone Cheeses

The provolone family is technically known as pasta filata (spun) cheese. The essential step in the preparation of these cheeses occurs after the separation of the curd from the whey. The curd is placed in either hot water or hot whey, which changes it into a stringy, plastic-like mass. The curd is then stretched, much the way taffy candy is stretched, and molded into the desired size and shape. Then it is salted by being soaked in brine, and following that, it may or may not be smoked.

The most commonly used member of this cheese family is provolone, which is slightly cured and usually smoked. It has a very important place in Italian cooking.

Mozzarella is another member of this cheese family, one that has become very well known in the United States because of the increased popularity of pizza. A fresh cheese, originally made of buffalo's milk, it originated in Italy just south of Rome. Buffalo-milk mozzarella is still sold in that area of Italy, but it is always made from cows' milk in the United States.

Originally, mozzarella was sold and consumed the day of manufacture, but with the advent of national distribution and commercial sale of the product, it no longer lends itself to that kind of treatment. However, mozzarella is still a fresh, uncured cheese. It is particularly adaptable to cooking, for it melts into a smooth, stringy mass desirable for such dishes as pizza and lasagne.

Scamorze cheese is a close relative of mozzarella. Both are fresh—uncured—and mild in flavor.

The Swiss Cheeses

Swiss is the second most popular variety of cheese in the United States, ranking just behind Cheddar. In Switzerland, its home country, this cheese is called Emmentaler, a name also used to some extent in the United States.

The distinguishing feature of Swiss cheese is its "eyes"—holes that develop throughout the cheese during ripening. These are the result of propionic acid bacteria that produce carbon dioxide bubbles throughout the body of the cheese. The size of the holes is controlled to some extent by regulating the temperature and time of ripening. Propionic acid bacteria also produce the characteristic sweet, nut-like flavor of Swiss cheese.

Gruyère is related to Swiss cheese, although the characteristic "eyes" are not as fully developed. A certain amount of surface growth is allowed to take place, resulting in a somewhat sharper flavor. Gruyère cheese is very popular in Europe, but has never gained similar popularity in the United States.

To avoid confusion, the cheese buyer should understand that Gruyère cheese as sold in the United States is a pasteurized process cheese (see page 103) containing Emmentaler and Gruyère. This is usually sold in small individually wrapped wedges and in round or half-round packages. It is not the same as the Gruyère found in Europe.

The Blue-Veined Cheeses

The blue-veined cheeses are characterized by the distribution of blue-green mold throughout the cheese, which results in a characteristic piquant flavor. This blue mold is the result of the inoculation of a strain of penicillium mold that grows throughout the body of the cheese.

Almost every cheese-consuming country of the world has developed a blue-veined cheese very similar to the blue cheese produced in the United States. The best known are Italy's Gorgonzola, England's Stilton, France's Roquefort and Denmark's Danablu.

All these blue cheeses with the exception of Roquefort are made of cows' milk. Roquefort is produced from sheep's milk in a region of southeastern

France and cured in the caves that occur in the same area.

During the manufacture of blue cheeses, the blue-mold powder (penicillium mold) is mixed with the curd either while it is in the vat or while it is being placed in molds or hoops. The cheese is held in these hoops for twenty-four hours.

After removal from the hoops, the cheese is salted over a period of approximately one week under conditions that simulate the temperature and humidity of the Roquefort caves. Approximately one week after salting, the cheese is mechanically pierced to produce holes that allow air penetration essential for mold growth. The cheese then cures for a period of about five months.

The Parmesan Cheeses

The members of this "hard-grating" cheese family, primarily associated with Italian cooking, were originally developed in Italy in the vicinity of Parma. They are grated and sprinkled on spaghetti, pizza, minestrone and tossed salads, and are used in baked dishes, such as veal parmigiana and lasagne.

These cheeses are characterized by their hard, granular texture, which makes them ideal for grating. In fact, much of the Parmesan and Romano cheese produced in the United States is sold grated or shredded, in jars or cardboard containers.

Parmesan is the most familiar cheese in this group and perhaps one of the best-known Italian cheeses in the United States. It is made from a mixture of whole and skim milk and is usually cured from fourteen to twenty-four months to develop the characteristic texture and piquant flavor.

Romano, the other member of the family well

known in the United States, originated in the Latium area near Rome. It is very similar to Parmesan cheese and is used in the same manner, but it has a sharper, more piquant flavor. Both Parmesan and Romano are excellent "seasoning cheeses."

The Fresh, Uncured Cheeses

The fresh cheeses do not follow exactly the six major steps of cheese manufacture. Coagulation of the curd is initiated by the addition of a lactic acid starter, with or without a small amount of rennet. Also, as their name implies, these cheeses are not cured, but are sold fresh. They have a mild flavor.

Cream cheese is an American original enjoyed since 1872. It starts as a mixture of milk and cream, which is pasteurized and coagulated by a starter. Originally the curd was poured into cloth bags and pressed to expel the whey. About 1945, Kraft perfected a method of removing the curd by centrifugal force. This procedure is the one primarily used today. It produces a fine, smooth-bodied cheese that has greater keeping qualities than cheese produced by the "bag method."

Neufchatel is the name of a lower-fat product similar to cream cheese. Because of their mild flavor and smooth, creamy texture, both cream cheese and Neufchatel blend readily with other ingredients and are used in a wide variety of recipes. They are especially popular as a base for many varieties of dips and spreads.

Cottage cheese is a third member of the family of fresh, uncured cheeses. In making cottage cheese, skim milk is coagulated by adding lactic acid starter and sometimes a small amount of rennet. When the curd is sufficiently firm, it is cut into cubes and heated in the whey. After the whey has been removed, the curd is washed and salted. Cottage cheese is usually creamed to improve its flavor and texture. This is done by adding a mixture of cream and milk. Cottage cheese can be purchased in small or large-curd form.

The Surface-Ripened Cheeses

 Members of the surface-ripened cheese family include Camembert, Brie, brick, Muenster, Bel Paese, Port du Salut and Limburger. These cheeses may be divided into two major groups, based upon the type of organisms that are used to produce the characteristic flavor. In the case of all surface-ripened cheeses, a bacterial culture or a mold culture is grown on the surface of the cheese. The enzymes produced by the growth of these organisms penetrate the cheese and bring about the development of the characteristic flavor and texture of each variety.

The two basic subfamilies within this large group of cheeses are differentiated by the type of organism used for ripening—mold or bacteria. Characteristic of the mold-ripened varieties are Camembert and Brie, both of which originated in France and both of which are very popular with cheese connoisseurs all over the world. The best-known variety of bacterial-ripened cheese is Limburger. Other popular cheeses of this type are Bel Paese of Italy and Port du Salut of France.

Brick and Muenster, which were originally members of this family of cheeses, can no longer be considered true members, for today they have little or no surface ripening. This is because of changes in consumer preferences for milder and milder versions of these cheeses.

The Whey Cheeses

 The whey group of cheeses is produced from whey rather than curd. These are not true cheeses, for whey is a by-product of cheese manufacture.

The whey cheeses vary greatly in characteristics. Perhaps the best-known cheese in this category is ricotta, used frequently in Italian cooking. Ricotta was originally produced by the coagulation of the albumen portion of the whey, which resulted in a soft, fresh cheese similar to cottage cheese. Today ricotta is made by the coagulation of a mixture of whey and whole or skim milk. It is a soft, grainy cheese, and can be purchased either dry or moist.

Two other cheeses of this family, gjetost and primost, are Scandinavian. They are prepared by condensing whey and adding small amounts of fat. Gjetost is rather hard; primost is a semisoft product. Another member of the family is sapsago, a Swiss type of whey cheese. It is the result of the acid coagulation of the protein in a mixture of skim milk, buttermilk and whey. The addition of the leaves of a cloverlike plant leads to the characteristic flavor and light green color. A hard cheese, it is primarily used grated.

Choosing a Favorite Cheese

Most of the members of the nine cheese families just discussed can be found in the dairy case at your supermarket. Browse through recipes to find interesting and unusual uses for the various kinds of cheeses that you and your family will enjoy.

On the following pages you will find a see-at-a-glance chart that will help you in identifying and buying the cheeses in the nine families and which will, hopefully, lead you to experiment with types with which you are not familiar.

The Cheese Families

	CHEESE	ORIGIN	CONSISTENCY AND TEXTURE	COLOR, SHAPE AND FLAVOR	BASIC INGREDIENT	RIPENING PERIOD
Cheddar Family	Cheddar	England	Hard; smooth, firm body	Light yellow to orange; varied shapes and styles with rind and rindless; mild to sharp	Cows' milk, whole	2-12 months or longer
	Colby	United States	Hard type, but softer and more open in texture than Cheddar	Light yellow to orange; cylindrical; mild	Cows' milk, whole	1-3 months
	Monterey (Jack)	United States	Semisoft; smooth, open texture	Creamy white wheels; mild	Cows' milk, whole	2-6 weeks for table use; 6-9 for grating
Dutch Family	Edam	Holland	Hard type, but softer than Cheddar; more open, mealy body	Creamy yellow with or without red wax coat: cannonball shape; mild, nutlike	Cows' milk, partly skimmed	2 months or longer
	Gouda	Holland	Hard type, but softer than Cheddar; more open, mealy body, like Edam	Creamy yellow with or without red wax coat: round and flat; mild, nutlike, similar to Edam	Cows' milk, partly skimmed but more milk fat than Edam	2-6 months
Provolone Family	Provolone	Italy	Hard; compact, flaky	Light golden yellow to golden brown, shiny surface bound with cord; yellowish white interior; pear, sausage and salami shapes; mild to sharp and piquant, usually smoked	Cows' milk, whole	2-12 months
	Mozzarella	Italy	Semisoft; plastic	Creamy white; rectangular and spherical; mild, delicate	Cows' milk, whole or partly skimmed	Unripened
	Scamorze	Italy	Semisoft; smooth	Light yellow; mild	Cows' milk, whole	Unripened

	CHEESE	ORIGIN	CONSISTENCY AND TEXTURE	COLOR, SHAPE AND FLAVOR	BASIC INGREDIENT	RIPENING PERIOD
Swiss Family	Swiss	Switzerland	Hard; smooth with large gas holes, or eyes	Rindless blocks and large wheels with rind; sweetish, nutlike	Cows' milk, partly skimmed	2 months minimum to 9 months or longer
	Gruyère	Switzerland	Hard; tiny gas holes, or eyes	Light yellow; flat wheels; sweetish, nutlike	Cows' milk, usually partly skimmed	3 months minimum
Blue Family	Blue	France	Semisoft; visible veins of mold; pasty, sometimes crumbly	White, marbled with blue-green mold; cylindrical; piquant, spicy	Cows' milk, whole	2 months minimum; 3-4 months usually; 9 months for pronounced flavor
	Gorgonzola	Italy	Semisoft; visible veins of mold; less moist than blue	Light tan surface, light yellow interior, marbled with blue-green mold; cylindrical; piquant, spicy, similar to blue	Cows' milk, whole, or goats' milk or mixture of these	3 months minimum
	Roquefort	France	Semisoft; visible veins of mold; pasty and sometimes crumbly	White marbled with blue-green mold; cylindrical, sharp, piquant, spicy	Sheep's milk	2 months minimum to 5 months or longer
	Stilton	England	Semisoft; visible veins of mold; slightly more crumbly than blue	White, marbled with blue-green mold; cylindrical; piquant, spicy, but milder than Roquefort	Cows' milk, whole with added cream	2-6 months or longer

	CHEESE	ORIGIN	CONSISTENCY AND TEXTURE	COLOR, SHAPE AND FLAVOR	BASIC INGREDIENT	RIPENING PERIOD
Parmesan Family	Parmesan (Reggiano)	Italy	Hard grating; granular, brittle body	Light yellow with brown or black coating; cylindrical: sharp, piquant	Cows' milk, partly skimmed	14 months minimum to 24 months or longer
	Romano	Italy	Hard; granular	Yellowish white interior, greenish black surface; sharp, piquant	Cows' milk	5 months minimum; 12 months for grating
Fresh, Uncured Family	Cream	United States	Soft; smooth, buttery	White, foil-wrapped in rectangular portions; mild, slightly acid	Cream and cows' milk, whole	Unripened
	Neufchatel	France	Soft; smooth, creamy	White; foil-wrapped in rectangular portions; mild	Cows' milk, whole	Unripened
	Cottage	Uncertain	Soft; moist, delicate, large or small curds	White; packaged in cuplike containers; mild, slightly acid	Cows' milk, skimmed; cream dressing may be added	Unripened
Surface-Ripened Family	Camembert	France	Soft; thin edible crust, creamy interior	White crust, creamy yellow interior; small wheels; mild to pungent	Cows' milk, whole	4-5 weeks
	Brie	France	Soft; thin edible crust, creamy interior	Whitish crust, creamy yellow interior; medium and small wheels; mild to pungent	Cows' milk, whole	4-8 weeks
	Brick	United States	Semisoft; smooth, waxy body	Light yellow to orange; brick-shaped; mild	Cows' milk, whole	2 weeks or longer
	Muenster	Germany	Semisoft; smooth, waxy body	Yellow, tan or white surface, creamy white interior; small wheels and blocks; mild to mellow, between brick and Limburger	Cows' milk, whole	2-8 weeks

	CHEESE	ORIGIN	CONSISTENCY AND TEXTURE	COLOR, SHAPE AND FLAVOR	BASIC INGREDIENT	RIPENING PERIOD
	Bel Paese	Italy	Soft; smooth, waxy body	Slightly gray surface, creamy yellow interior; small wheels; mild to moderately robust	Cows' milk, whole	6-8 weeks
	Port du Salut (Oka)	Trappist monasteries, France and Canada	Semisoft; smooth, buttery	Russet surface, creamy yellow interior; small wheels; mellow to robust, between Cheddar and Limburger	Cows' milk, whole or slightly acid	6-8 weeks
	Limburger	Belgium	Soft; smooth, waxy body	Creamy white; rectangular; robust, highly aromatic	Cows' milk, whole or partly skimmed	1-2 months
Whey Family	Gjetost	Norway	Hard; buttery	Golden brown; cubical and rectangular; sweetish, caramel	Whey from goats' milk	Unripened
	Primost	Norway	Semisoft	Light brown; cubical and cylindrical; mild, sweetish, caramel	Whey with added buttermilk, whole milk or cream	Unripened
	Sapsago	Switzerland	Hard grating; granular	Light green; small, cone-shaped; flavored with clover leaves, sweetish	Cows' milk, skimmed and soured, plus buttermilk and whey	5 months minimum
	Ricotta	Italy	Soft; moist and grainy, or dry	White; packaged fresh in paper, plastic or metal containers or dry for grating; bland, but semisweet	Whey and whole or skim milk, or whole or part skim milk	Unripened

Cheese Beginnings in America

In this country, cheese-making started not long after the Pilgrims landed at Plymouth Rock—in 1624, to be exact, right after the colonists, sick of their scant and tiresome diet, joyously welcomed the first cows to the new land. In 1801, President Thomas Jefferson was presented with a mammoth 1,235-pound cheese, and it was from awe at that monster that the catch-phrase "big cheese" arose. Cheese was then generally a home and farm product. There were few cheese factories. One of the first was a Cheddar factory, built by one Jesse Williams in 1851, at Oneida, New York.

By the time the manufacture of cheese became a thriving industry in the United States, the usual method of sale was for the producer—sometimes a wholesaler—to send his cheese to market in some central location (almost all cities had large outdoor or indoor markets) which the retailer would visit to choose those products he wanted to sell in his store.

Young Man with an Idea

In 1903, a young man named James L. Kraft had an idea—why not take the cheese to the retailer instead of making the retailer come to the cheese? He had, to begin with, a horse (his name was Paddy), a wagon and a working capital of sixty-five dollars—and abounding energy and a boundless imagination. He filled his wagon with cheese at the market, clucked to Paddy, and started making the rounds of Chicago grocers to sell them cheese.

But habit-bound Chicago grocers were unimpressed. They wiped their hands on long white aprons, twisted the ends of their handlebar moustaches and said, "Well, I don't know...."

Some days the total sales added up to less than

ten dollars. On such days, J. L. held "business con-
ferences" with Paddy, who gave an occasional twitch
of his ears in reply.

One day, J. L. explained to Paddy that they had
been careless and forgetful. "From now on, Paddy,"
he told his horse, "we're going to work with God as
our Partner."

Business Begins to Improve

With his wagon hitched to this star, business began
to improve, and J. L. and Paddy became the historic
"co-founders" of the Kraft Foods Company.

In August of 1904, J. L. wrote to a friend: "To
give you an idea of what you would have to do should
things work out all right: It is simply a grocery route
on a large scale. You take a horse and wagon (and my
wagons are fancy ones) and get customers that you
can call on once or twice a week and supply them regu-
larly. I am driving one wagon myself, and I am taking
care of the horses myself, but if all goes well, I think I
will have four horses by Christmas . . ."

As time went by, J. L.'s business flourished and
prospered. Not only did he do well, but he learned a
great deal about cheese. He learned, for example, that
there were problems in the manufacture and distribution of cheese—many of those problems connected
with keeping qualities. Although natural cheese has
a longer life—both in the store and in the home—than,
for instance, the milk from which it is made, it is per-
ishable in degrees varying with the kind of cheese.
The very ripening processes which produce the different varieties, textures and flavors of natural cheese
don't stop when the particular cheese has reached its
prime, and presently deterioration and drying set in.

Aside from those problems, variations in the

handling and curing of cheese cause appreciable differences in taste and texture. In other words, two cheeses of the same brand, same variety and same age might not necessarily *be* the same.

J. L. Buys a Double Boiler

There ought to be some way to lick those problems, James Kraft decided—and shortly thereafter found himself in the cheese-making, as well as the cheese-marketing, business. He began to experiment (in an ordinary kitchen double boiler, price, fifty-nine cents) with blended cheeses, and later with the pasteurizing and blending of cheese, as solutions to these difficulties. There were early failures but, eventually, success. In 1916, the method of producing process cheese was patented by J. L. Kraft.

By 1917, Kraft cheese in tins, a pasteurized process product, was ready for the market. By 1920, Kraft's five-pound loaf, a pasteurized, blended cheese in a wooden container, was placed on sale, and became an immediate, spectacular success.

Pasteurized Process Cheese Products

Process cheese is a product manufactured from natural cheese according to specified government standards, and has had a major influence on the eating habits of the nation.

The processing of natural cheese provides a more stable product with greater uniformity of flavor and texture. Processing consists of blending various natural cheeses—mild, sharp and extra sharp—by heating with the aid of an emulsifier. The result is a homogeneous product consistent in flavor, body and texture.

The manufacture of process cheese is quality

controlled throughout to ensure uniform good flavor, smooth texture, melting properties and high nutrition. Available in a variety of types, shapes and flavors, process cheese can be counted on to give excellent results in cooking.

The most common natural cheeses used for processing are Cheddar and Swiss. There is often some confusion as to the differentiation of the various process cheese products—pasteurized process *cheese*, cheese *food* and cheese *spread*. The major differences in these products are shown in this chart:

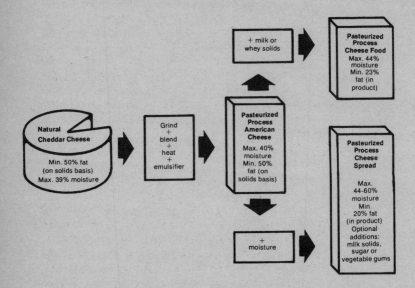

Pasteurized Process Cheese

Natural cheese is always the start for processed cheese products. Natural cheeses of various ages and characteristics are selected and laboratory tested to assure the desired quality in the finished process cheese. Grinding or blending of the cheese by machine follows; the blend is then transferred to the cooker.

Emulsifiers, designated by established government standards, are added during the cooking. Emulsifiers prevent separation of the fat during processing and produce a cheese with the proper melting and slicing properties.

Pasteurization in the manufacture of process cheese, as in the case of milk, consists of the application of heat. Following established standards, the cheese is pasteurized at a temperature of not less than 150° F. for at least thirty seconds. This step prevents further aging of the natural cheeses.

Packing is the final step. From the cooker the hot, smooth, semiliquid cheese flows to a filling machine, where precisely weighed amounts are poured into containers lined with moisture-proof material to form loaves. For packaged slices, the cheese is run over chilled rollers where it forms ribbons of uniform width. These ribbons run onto a conveyor where they are stacked, cut and packaged in one continuous operation.

Pasteurized Process Cheese Food

During the making of a natural cheese, some nutrients of milk remain in the whey when it is drained from the curd. These nutrients can be returned to the hot cheese during the pasteurization operation. They are usually added in the form of concentrates or powders of skim milk and whey. When these milk solids are added to process cheese, the amount of fat is reduced and the moisture content is increased; then the product becomes pasteurized process *cheese food*.

For variety, other ingredients, such as meats, vegetables and fruits, may be added.

Pasteurized process cheese foods are milder in flavor and melt more readily than both natural and pasteurized process cheese.

Pasteurized Process Cheese Spread

When a softer, more spreadable cheese product is desired, other ingredients may be added to process cheese, such as milk products, sweetening agents and vegetable gums. These products normally have a somewhat higher moisture and lower fat content than do pasteurized process cheese and pasteurized process cheese food. They are referred to as pasteurized process *cheese spreads*. Again, as with cheese foods, other ingredients can be added to broaden the flavor range—such ingredients as pimiento, olives, peppers, spices and flavoring.

Why Cheese in Your Daily Diet?

Cheese—as is the milk from which it is produced—is considered a nearly perfect food, providing a great many of the essential food elements that the body needs, such as protein, minerals, vitamins and fat. Cheese is one of the most nutritious, concentrated and palatable of foods—most nutrition experts consider cheese, a highly concentrated protein food, to be one of the basic foods.

There are three milk proteins: casein, albumin and globulin. Casein, the most important of the proteins, can be found only in milk. It is considered a complete protein because it contains all the necessary amino acids, the building blocks from which all proteins are made. The essential amino acids are indispensable in the diet because the body cannot synthe-

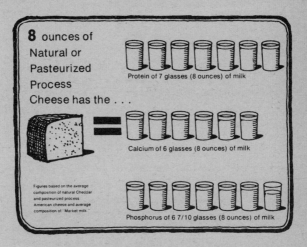

8 ounces of
Natural or
Pasteurized
Process
Cheese has the . . .

Protein of 7 glasses (8 ounces) of milk

Calcium of 6 glasses (8 ounces) of milk

Figures based on the average
composition of natural Cheddar
and pasteurized process
American cheese and average
composition of "Market milk"

Phosphorus of 6 7/10 glasses (8 ounces) of milk

size them at the rate needed to maintain life and support growth and tissue repair. Nonessential amino acids can be formed by the body at a sufficient rate.

Proteins from various food sources differ in their nutritive value because of differences in amino acid content. A large share of the protein in the diet, especially for rapidly growing children and adolescents, should come from the complete, high quality protein foods. Cheese is such a food, containing significant amounts of essential and nonessential amino acids.

Cheese is also a readily digested food. Experiments have shown that from 90 to 99 percent of the nutrients in cheese are digested. Nutritionists rank cheese among the best of protein foods, even for very young children. It is also an excellent source of calcium and phosphorus. Though varieties of cheese differ somewhat in composition, cheese is a good source of vitamin A and contains significant amounts of the water-soluble B vitamins in milk, although it is not considered a primary source for these nutrients. The fats present in cheese are all butterfats with the same nutritional properties as the butterfats in cream and milk.

Adventures in the World of Cheese

A taste tour of the fascinating world of cheese begins at the dairy case in your neighborhood supermarket. Cheese products based on centuries of tradition are readily available, offering a vast array of taste and texture for you to sample. With flavors that range from mild to sharp and textures that go from soft and smooth to hard and coarse, there are cheeses to suit every palate.

Cheese offers eating enjoyment, and it is nutritionally a near-perfect food, two excellent reasons for making cheese play a big role in your meal planning and snack making.

Knowing the fine points of buying and storing cheese, as well as employing a variety of menu uses, will increase the enjoyment of cheese and pay big dividends in good nutrition for the whole family.

Discovering Your Favorites

With all those varieties of cheese available—over 2,000, some dairy scientists say—how do you find the ones you and your family will like best? Be adventurous! Try new kinds. Sample cheeses you've heard about but never tasted. Introduce your family to different varieties in daily menus. Consult cookbooks and the food pages of your newspaper for ideas on how to use cheese to make meals for the family and for guests more interesting, more nutritious. Browse in the dairy case at your supermarket to become familiar with the many kinds of cheese available. Notice, too, the convenient forms in which cheese is available—slices, sticks, wedges, shredded and grated, ready to help you put together dishes that will have the family asking for seconds.

Cheese Buying Guide

When you start out to buy cheese, the first thing to remember is that there are, as you have learned, two major categories: natural cheese and process cheese. Perhaps you'll want to take the chart of natural cheeses (beginning on page 95) with you to guide you in choosing varieties new to you.

Cold-pack or club cheese is natural cheese ground and blended to be uniformly softer and more spreadable at room temperature. It has the characteristic flavor of the natural cheese from which it is made and can be purchased plain or as a blend of the cheese with fruits, vegetables, spices or wines.

Pasteurized process cheese is always made from natural cheeses ground and blended and heated with the aid of an emulsifier to make a cheese of uniform quality, flavor, texture and body. Process cheese is milder in flavor and softer in body than the natural cheese from which it is derived, and it keeps better because pasteurization stops the curing or ripening process. It is ideally suited for cooking, as it melts readily and smoothly.

Pasteurized process cheese food is a variation of pasteurized process cheese, found today in links and individually wrapped slices. It differs from pasteurized process cheese in that milk or whey solids have been added. Pasteurized process cheese foods are milder in flavor, have a softer body and melt more readily than either natural or pasteurized process cheese because of their higher moisture and lower fat content. Meat, fruits, vegetables or flavoring may be added to lend variety.

Pasteurized process cheese spread is another pasteurized process cheese variation—milk solids and certain other flavoring foods, such as pimiento or bacon bits, may be added. It is normally higher in moisture and lower in fat than pasteurized process cheese or cheese food. Its smooth texture, pleasingly mild flavor and high nutritional qualities make it a cheese product that pleases the whole family.

Cheese Buymanship

Look for natural cheese and process cheese products in or near the refrigerated dairy case at your supermarket. Buy cheese products to suit the family's needs. When planning daily menus, remember that cheese, a nearly perfect food, fits into two of the basic food groups—the milk group and the meat group.

Natural cheeses are always stored in the dairy case, where they tempt the eye in an array of distinctive shapes: wedges, wheels, balls, flat rounds, loaves, sticks and convenient packaged slices. Individually wrapped slices are a recent, most important breakthrough, as they assure freshness and longer storage time.

Pasteurized process cheese foods and spreads are also available in wide variety: slices, loaves, links, dips and spreads. The process cheese products in glasses, loaves and squeeze packs that do not require refrigeration are found above or near the dairy case.

How to Store Cheese

When storing unopened cheese at home, consult the label for manufacturer's instructions or follow the lead of your supermarket and store the product as it was stored there when you bought it.

You'll find most cheeses in the dairy case—your clue to refrigerate them at home. Jars and loaves that are kept on nonrefrigerated shelves can be stored at room temperature at home until used—once opened, they should be kept in the refrigerator. Some products, such as squeeze packs, are the exceptions; these should never be refrigerated. They'll stay fresh at room temperature as long as they last.

"Keep air out and moisture in" is a good rule to remember when storing cheese. Reseal unused portions in the original wrapping or use foil, plastic bags or transparent wrap snug and tight against the cheese, to keep it moist and fresh. Individually wrapped single slices of cheese, carefully designed foil packaging materials and easy-to-open-and-reseal plastic lids and metal caps are designed to keep cheese products fresh.

Occasionally surface mold may form on cheese even when it has been properly stored. This mold is harmless and will not affect the quality or flavor of the cheese. Simply cut off the mold and enjoy the rest of the cheese. Remember that the blue cheese family gets its piquant flavor from the characteristic blue-green mold throughout the cheese.

To Freeze or Not to Freeze

If properly stored, cheese keeps a relatively long period of time at refrigerator temperature. Freezing cheese will extend its storage life, but may affect the body and texture. Frozen cheese may become crumbly or mealy, and is then best suited for cooking.

For best results, cheese should be tightly sealed in moisture-proof material, such as plastic wrap or foil especially designed for freezing. Cheeses such as Cheddar, Swiss, Edam or Gouda can be stored in the freezer if frozen rapidly in small (half pound) packages. If the cheese has been cut into small cubes, keep it in the freezer no longer than three weeks. Slices and loaves of natural cheese, such as Cheddar and Swiss, and pasteurized process cheese products may be kept frozen for up to three months. Before using cheese, thaw slowly, preferably in the refrigerator while still in its wrapping.

Cheese at Its Best

Other than in hot dishes, the flavor and character of all cheeses, except cottage, Neufchatel and cream cheese, come through best when served at room temperature. To fully enjoy the special qualities of a cheese, remove it from the refrigerator at least thirty minutes before it will be served. Cheeses such as Camembert should be soft and almost runny to be at their most pleasing, so remove them from the refrigerator at least a couple of hours in advance. Serve cottage, Neufchatel and cream cheeses chilled.

Shredded versus Grated

When used for melting—as in sauces or for toppings or in other cooked forms, such as casseroles—cheese should be shredded unless you are using pasteurized process cheese spread or pasteurized process cheese food, both of which melt satisfactorily in a liquid medium when sliced or cubed. Some cheeses are available preshredded in jars and in film packages. To shred cheese at home, use the coarse openings of your grater and you'll produce the long strips or shreds of cheese desirable for cooking purposes.

How Much Cheese?

When a recipe calls for a specific measure of cheese— a cup or a half cup, for example—it's easy to know how much to buy. Just keep in mind that one-quarter pound—four ounces—of cheese is equal to one cup shredded cheese. This rule applies whether you are using any one of the many varieties of cheese in its natural form or pasteurized process cheese in any of its forms.

About Cooking with Cheese

Like all protein foods, cheese is adversely affected by high heat or prolonged cooking. Although pasteurized process cheese products are less susceptible to heat than natural cheese, it is advisable to follow these two rules of cheese cookery:

1. Use low to medium heat.
2. Do not overcook—heat just until cheese melts.

* When adding to hot foods, shred natural cheese and cube or slice process cheese.

* When making a sauce, add cheese at the end of cooking time and heat just until melted.

* When broiling, place pan so that cheese is several inches below heat source; broil just until cheese melts.

* When cheese is used in baked dishes, bake at low (325° F.) to moderate (375° F.) temperatures.

* When topping a casserole, place cheese on top for the last few minutes of baking.

* Four ounces of natural or process cheese equals 1 cup shredded or cubed cheese.

* Shred natural cheese that is to be melted in sauces, toppings or other foods. (Cheese can also be purchased already shredded in convenient packages.)

* Cube process cheese products when adding to other foods. It will melt quickly and blend easily.

* Parmesan type cheeses are usually grated or shredded. Grated is finer and drier than shredded.

* Cream cheese and Neufchatel blend readily with other ingredients if first allowed to soften at room temperature.

Adventures in Cheese Cookery

* Crumble blue or Roquefort cheese into your favorite salad dressing.

* Stir cubes of cream cheese or Velveeta cheese spread or shredded Cracker Barrel Cheddar into scrambled eggs the last few minutes of cooking.

* Toss cubes of Velveeta or Cracker Barrel cheese with fruit or vegetable salads.

* Top broiled hamburgers with pasteurized process cheese food slices, natural cheese slices or crumbled blue cheese. Broil just until cheese melts.

* Parmesan is the "seasoning cheese." Use it grated or shredded in sauces, soups and salads; on breads to be heated in the oven or grilled; on hot cooked vegetables or pasta.

* Top hot fruit desserts, such as cobblers, deep-dish pies and fruit compotes, with whipped cream cheese.

* Mozzarella or scamorze, the pizza cheeses, are also excellent in other traditional Italian dishes—lasagne, canneloni, veal parmigiana.

A Last Word

Kraft's continuing experimentation and research have resulted in an increasing number of wonderful products whose names have become household words and whose flavors and various properties of slicing, shredding, melting, grating and spreading have become the joy of good cooks everywhere. Pasteurized process cheese food in glasses, various kinds of ready-sliced cheese in packages, cream cheese guaranteed fresh when you buy it, individually wrapped cheese and process cheese slices—these are only a few of Kraft's contributions to ease of preparation, ease of serving and joy of eating in American homes.

—The Editors

Sandwiches, Snacks and Other Quick-to-Fix Delights

First they call, "Mom, I'm home!" and right on the heels of that, "Mom, I'm hungry!" Here are cheese snacks and sandwiches to build you a reputation as the best cook on the block, not only with the youngsters but with the grown-ups, as well.

Hearty Picnic Sticks

*Cheez Whiz Pasteurized
Process Cheese Spread
Salami slices
Bread sticks*

Spread Cheez Whiz on salami;
wrap around bread sticks.

Miniburgers

*1 8-ounce can refrigerated
biscuits
Margarine
1 pound ground beef
¼ cup dry bread crumbs
1 egg, beaten
1 teaspoon instant minced onion
½ teaspoon salt
¼ teaspoon pepper
¼ teaspoon garlic salt
Nippy Brand Sharp Pasteurized
Process Cheese Food, link,
sliced
10 cherry tomatoes, cut in half*

Prepare biscuits as directed on
package; split. Spread with
margarine; toast. Combine
ground beef, bread crumbs, egg
and seasonings; shape into 20
patties. Broil until browned on
both sides. Top each patty with
cheese food slice and tomato
half. Broil until cheese food begins to melt. Place beef patty
on biscuit half. 20 snacks.

Jubilee Eggs

*1 dozen hard-cooked eggs
1 5-ounce jar Kraft Pimento
Pasteurized Neufchatel
Cheese Spread
2 tablespoons mayonnaise
2 tablespoons chopped green
pepper
½ teaspoon salt*

Cut eggs in half lengthwise.
Mash yolks; blend with cheese
spread and mayonnaise. Add
green pepper and salt. Refill egg
whites. 24 egg halves.

Calypso Kabobs

*Smokelle Pasteurized Process
Cheese Food, link
Nippy Brand Sharp Pasteurized
Process Cheese Food, link
Salami slices
Sliced celery
Sliced carrots
Sliced mushrooms
Apples, cubed
Mandarin orange sections*

Cut each link into thick slices;
cut each slice in quarters. Alternate slices of Smokelle, salami,
celery, carrots and mushrooms
or Nippy, salami, apples and
oranges on skewers or picks.

French-Wiches

*8 slices sandwich bread
1 6-ounce package Kraft
American Singles Pasteurized
Process Cheese Food
Tomato slices
Dill pickle slices
Onion slices
1 egg, slightly beaten
⅓ cup milk
3 tablespoons margarine*

For each sandwich, cover slice of bread with slice of cheese food, tomato, pickle, onion and second slice of cheese food and bread. Combine egg and milk; dip each sandwich in mixture. Melt margarine in skillet. Grill sandwich over low heat until golden brown on each side. 4 sandwiches.

Sicilian Steak Sandwiches

*6 cube steaks
2 tablespoons margarine
1 large green pepper, cut
in strips
¼ cup Italian-style dressing
1 large onion, sliced
1 large tomato, sliced
6 individual French loaves,
split
Kraft Natural Low Moisture
Part-Skim Mozzarella Cheese
Slices, cut in quarters*

Cook meat in margarine. Cook green pepper in dressing 5 minutes. Add onion and tomato; continue cooking 5 minutes. For each sandwich, place meat on bottom half of loaf; cover with vegetables. Top with cheese slices; broil until cheese melts. Serve with top half of loaf. 6 sandwiches.

Monte Cristo Sandwiches

*3 eggs, slightly beaten
⅓ cup milk
12 slices sandwich bread
Kraft Natural Swiss Cheese
Slices, cut in half
6 boiled ham slices
Margarine
Confectioners' sugar
Currant jelly*

Heat oven to 425°. Combine eggs and milk. For each sandwich, cover slice of bread with slice of cheese, ham and second slice of cheese. Top with second slice of bread. Dip each sandwich in egg mixture; brown on both sides in margarine. Bake at 425°, 15 minutes. Sprinkle with sugar. Serve with jelly. 6 sandwiches.

Tote 'n Grill Sandwich

*1 loaf Vienna bread, cut in
½-inch slices
Boiled ham slices
Pickle and pimiento loaf slices
Bologna slices
Tomato slices
Onion slices
Green pepper rings
Kraft Pasteurized Process
American Cheese Slices
Kraft Pasteurized Process
Pimento Cheese Slices
Margarine*

For each sandwich, cover one slice of bread with slices of meat, tomato, onion, green pepper and cheese; top with second slice of bread. Secure each sandwich with toothpick. Spread outside of each sandwich with margarine; place sandwiches close together to form a loaf. Wrap in aluminum foil; grill 10 to 15 minutes.

Turkey Sandwiches Bombay

2 cups chopped cooked turkey
½ cup raisins
½ cup salted peanuts, chopped
½ cup chopped celery
¼ cup chopped onion
Mayonnaise
¼ teaspoon curry powder
16 slices white bread
1 12-ounce package Kraft American Singles Pasteurized Process Cheese Food

Combine turkey, raisins, peanuts, celery, onion and enough mayonnaise to moisten. Add curry powder; mix well. For each sandwich, cover slice of bread with cheese food slice. Top with turkey salad, second cheese food slice and second slice of bread. 8 sandwiches.

Doggie-Burgers

1 pound ground beef
1 teaspoon salt
¼ teaspoon pepper
3 frankfurters, cut in half lengthwise
Barbecue sauce
Kraft Pasteurized Process American Cheese Slices, cut in triangles
6 frankfurter buns, split
Prepared mustard
Dill pickle slices

Combine beef and seasonings. Form beef around half of frankfurter to fit frankfurter bun. Brush with barbecue sauce; broil to desired doneness. Top with cheese; return to broiler until cheese begins to melt. For each sandwich, spread bottom half of bun with mustard. Cover with pickle slices, meat and top half of bun. 6 sandwiches.

Bountiful Beef Sandwich

Sliced Italian bread
Sliced roast beef
Kraft Natural Brick Cheese Slices
Tomato slices
Bacon Horseradish Sauce

For each sandwich, cover slice of bread with slices of beef, cheese and tomato. Top with Bacon Horseradish Sauce.

Bacon Horseradish Sauce

½ cup mayonnaise
1 4-ounce container Kraft
Whipped Cream Cheese with
Bacon and Horseradish
¼ teaspoon dry mustard
Dash each of salt, cayenne and
paprika

Gradually add mayonnaise to whipped cream cheese, mixing until well blended. Stir in remaining ingredients. 1 cup.

Savory Sloppy Joes

1 pound ground beef
1 cup barbecue sauce
¼ cup chopped green pepper
¼ cup chopped onion
8 hamburger buns, split
Velveeta Pasteurized Process
Cheese Spread, sliced

Brown meat; drain. Add barbecue sauce, green pepper and onion. Cover; cook 15 minutes. For each sandwich, spoon meat mixture onto bottom half of bun; cover with Velveeta slices. Broil until Velveeta begins to melt. Serve with top half of bun. 8 sandwiches.

Buckaroo Franks

½ pound Velveeta Pasteurized
Process Cheese Spread, cubed
½ cup chopped green onion
6 frankfurter buns, split,
toasted
Margarine
6 frankfurters, cooked
Crushed potato chips

Heat Velveeta over low heat; stir until smooth. Add onion. For each sandwich, spread bottom half of bun with margarine; top with frankfurter. Cover with Velveeta sauce. Sprinkle generously with potato chips. Cover with top half of bun. 6 sandwiches.

Hearty Danish

Sliced rye bread
Mayonnaise
Lettuce
Kraft Natural Swiss Cheese
Slices
Tomato slices
Sliced cooked turkey
Kraft Natural Caraway Cheese
Slices
Crisply cooked bacon slices

For each sandwich, spread bread with mayonnaise; top with lettuce. Cover with slices of Swiss cheese, tomatoes, turkey, Caraway cheese and bacon.

Devonshire Muffins

English muffins, split, toasted
Salad dressing
Tomato slices
Kraft Natural Caraway Cheese
Slices, cut in half
Crisply cooked bacon slices

Spread muffin halves with salad dressing. Cover each with slice of tomato and cheese; broil until cheese melts. Top with bacon.

Opposite: Savory Sloppy Joes

Cheeseburgers

Hot cooked hamburger patties
Kraft Pasteurized Process
American Cheese Slices
Hamburger buns, split,
toasted

For each sandwich, cover patty with cheese slice; broil until melted. Place patty on bottom half of bun; cover with top half of bun.

Other ways: Bayside Cheeseburgers—Cover patty with cheese slice; broil until melted. Top with avocado and ripe olive slices. Place patty on bottom half of bun. Bronco Cheeseburgers—Cover patty with cheese slice and French-fried onions; broil until cheese melts. Spread bottom half of bun with catsup; cover with patty and top half of bun. Cheeseburgers Chow Mein—Cover patty with cheese slice; broil until melted. Spread bottom half of bun with salad dressing and dill pickle relish; cover with patty, chow mein noodles and top half of bun. Cheeseburgers Royal Fare—Cover bottom half of bun with cheese slice, hamburger patty and second slice of cheese; broil

until cheese melts. Top with tomato slices, pickle slices and top half of bun. Swiss Burgers—Cover patty with slice of Kraft Natural Swiss Cheese Slices, cut in half. Broil until melted. Spread bottom half of bun with prepared mustard; cover with patty and top half of bun.

Stateside Danish

French bread, sliced
Salad dressing
Kraft Natural Cheddar Cheese
Slices
Sliced roast beef, rolled
Tomato slices
Green pepper rings, cut in
half
Onion rings

For each sandwich, spread bread with salad dressing. Top with slice of cheese and roast beef. Garnish with tomato, green pepper and onion.

Grilled Reuben Sandwiches

Sliced rye bread
Kraft Natural Swiss Cheese
Slices, cut in half
Thinly sliced corned beef
Sauerkraut, drained
Soft margarine

Cover one slice of bread with cheese slice, corned beef, sauerkraut and second slice of bread. Spread with margarine; grill on both sides until lightly browned.

Peppy Provolone Burgers

1 pound ground beef
1 8-ounce can tomato sauce
⅓ cup Kraft Grated Parmesan
*   Cheese*
¼ cup chopped onion
¼ cup chopped ripe olives
1½ teaspoons salt
½ teaspoon oregano
4 hamburger buns, split
2 6-ounce packages Kraft
Natural Provolone Cheese
*   Slices*

Combine meat, tomato sauce, Parmesan cheese, onion, olives and seasonings; mix well. Spread mixture on halves of buns; broil 12 to 15 minutes, 4 inches from heat. Top with Provolone cheese slices; return to broiler until cheese melts. Serve open-faced. Garnish with green pepper rings and cherry peppers, if desired. 8 sandwiches.

Malibu Burgers

2 pounds ground beef
Salt and pepper
*   *   *   *   *
1 cup dairy sour cream
¼ cup finely chopped onion
2 tablespoons chopped parsley
1 cup (4 ounces) shredded
Cracker Barrel Brand Sharp
Natural Cheddar Cheese
6 slices dark rye bread, toasted
Soft margarine
Lettuce
2 large tomatoes, sliced

Shape meat into 6 oval patties; broil on both sides to desired doneness. Season to taste. Mix together sour cream, onion and parsley. Top each hamburger patty with sour cream mixture and cheese; broil until cheese melts. For each sandwich, spread slice of toast with margarine; top with lettuce, tomato slices and hamburger patty. Garnish with pitted ripe olive and cocktail onion on pick, if desired. 6 sandwiches.

Country Squire Sandwiches

4 slices rye bread
Margarine
1 cup shredded lettuce
Cracker Barrel Brand Sharp
Natural Cheddar Cheese,
*   sliced*
Sliced cooked chicken
Tomato slices
4 hard-cooked eggs, sliced
Canterbury Dressing
1 avocado, sliced

For each sandwich, spread slice of bread with margarine; cover with lettuce, cheese, chicken, tomato and egg slices. Top with Canterbury Dressing and avocado slices. 4 sandwiches.

Canterbury Dressing

⅔ cup dairy sour cream
⅓ cup mayonnaise
1 teaspoon garlic salt

Combine ingredients; mix until well blended. Chill. 1 cup.

Circle Burgers

1 pound ground beef
1 teaspoon salt
2 English muffins, split,
toasted
Prepared mustard
Cheez Whiz Pasteurized
Process Cheese Spread

Combine meat and salt; form into 4 doughnut-shaped patties. Broil on both sides to desired doneness. For each sandwich, spread half of muffin with mustard; top with patty. Spoon Cheez Whiz into center of patty. 4 sandwiches.

Empire Turkey Sandwiches

1 cup milk
1 8-ounce package Philadelphia
Brand Cream Cheese
½ cup Kraft Grated Parmesan
Cheese
¼ teaspoon salt
¼ teaspoon garlic salt
6 slices white bread, toasted
6 slices hot cooked turkey
Paprika

Gradually add milk to softened cream cheese, mixing until well blended. Heat slowly; stir in Parmesan cheese and seasonings. For each sandwich, top slice of toast with slice of turkey; cover with sauce. Sprinkle with paprika. 6 sandwiches.

Royal Canadian Sandwiches

½ pound Tasty Brand Imitation
Pasteurized Process Cheese
Spread, cubed
½ cup skim milk
½ teaspoon prepared mustard
¼ teaspoon Worcestershire
sauce
3 English muffins, split,
toasted
12 slices cooked Canadian
bacon
6 unsweetened or artificially
sweetened pineapple slices

Combine Tasty Brand, milk, mustard and Worcestershire sauce. Stir over low heat until sauce is smooth. Cover each muffin half with 2 slices Canadian bacon and 1 pineapple slice. Top with sauce. 6 sandwiches.

Beachcomber Sandwiches

Individual French loaves, split
Mayonnaise
Lettuce
Boiled ham slices
Kraft Bacon Pasteurized
Process Cheese Food, link,
sliced
Nippy Brand Sharp Pasteurized
Process Cheese Food,
link, sliced

For each sandwich, spread bottom half of loaf with mayonnaise; cover with lettuce and layers of ham and cheese food slices. Serve with top half of loaf.

Toasty Cheese 'n Beef Stack-ups

Hard rolls, split
Kraft Whipped Cream Cheese with Onion
Thinly sliced roast beef
Tomato slices

For each sandwich, spread bottom half of roll with whipped cream cheese; broil until cheese puffs. Top with beef and tomato slices. Serve with top half of roll.

Frosted Sandwich Loaf

1 1-pound loaf unsliced sandwich bread
Margarine
2 8-ounce packages Philadelphia Brand Cream Cheese
¼ cup finely chopped watercress
Dash of salt and pepper
Egg Salad
Ham Salad
⅓ cup milk

Remove crusts from bread. Cut into 4 lengthwise slices; spread with margarine. Combine ⅓ package softened cream cheese, watercress and seasonings, mixing until well blended. Spread one slice of bread with Egg Salad; cover with a second slice spread with cream cheese mixture. Top with third slice of bread spread with Ham Salad and remaining slice of bread. Combine remaining softened cream cheese and milk, mixing until well blended. Frost sandwich loaf. 12 servings.

Egg Salad

3 hard-cooked eggs, finely chopped
½ teaspoon prepared mustard
¼ teaspoon salt
Dash of pepper
Mayonnaise

Combine eggs, mustard, seasonings and enough mayonnaise to moisten; mix lightly.

Ham Salad

1 cup ground cooked ham
2 tablespoons chopped sweet pickles
Mayonnaise

Combine ham, pickles and enough mayonnaise to moisten; mix lightly.

Tangy Long Loaf

1 1-pound loaf unsliced
white bread
⅓ cup soft margarine
¼ cup finely chopped onion
1 tablespoon poppy seeds
2 teaspoons prepared mustard
Dash of Tabasco sauce
1 8-ounce package Old English
Sharp Pasteurized Process
American Cheese Slices

Heat oven to 350°. Divide loaf into nine equal parts, cutting through to within ½-inch of bottom of loaf. Combine margarine, onion, poppy seeds, mustard and Tabasco; mix well. Reserve about 2 tablespoons of mixture. Spread remaining mixture on one half of the cut surfaces of the bread. Place one slice of cheese in each slit. Spread reserved mixture on top of bread. Place bread on baking sheet; bake at 350°, 15 to 20 minutes.

Cheesy Long Loaf

1 loaf French bread
Soft margarine
Kraft Pasteurized Process
American Cheese Slices, cut
in half diagonally

Heat oven to 400°. Slash bread diagonally at 1-inch intervals; spread slices with margarine. Wrap loaf in aluminum foil; bake at 400°, 15 minutes. Insert cheese in slashes; return to oven until cheese melts.

Seacoast Special

1½ cups (6½-ounce can)
crabmeat, drained, flaked
Mayonnaise
2 teaspoons chili sauce
4 slices white bread, toasted
Margarine
Lettuce
4 Kraft Pasteurized Process
American Cheese Slices

Combine crabmeat with enough mayonnaise to moisten. Add chili sauce; mix lightly. For each sandwich, spread slice of toast with margarine; cover with lettuce, cheese slice and crabmeat mixture. Garnish with watercress or parsley, if desired. 4 sandwiches.

Big Hero Sandwich

French bread, cut in half
lengthwise
Coleslaw
Salami slices
Kraft Pasteurized Process
American Cheese Slices
Boiled ham slices
Green pepper rings
Crisply cooked bacon slices
Hard-cooked eggs, sliced

Heat oven to 325°. Cover bottom half of bread with coleslaw. Add layers of salami, cheese, ham and second layer of cheese. Top with green pepper rings and bacon. Bake at 325° until cheese melts. Garnish with egg slices. Serve with top half of bread.
Nice to know: This sandwich can also be served cold.

A Bounty of Breads

Here's a whole set of new ideas to fill your house with
the heavenly aroma of home baking—quicker-than-quick
breads, yeast breads and other treats that are fun
to make—all of them better for the cheese that's in them.

Coffee-Time Cake

1 8-ounce package Philadelphia
Brand Cream Cheese
½ cup margarine
1¼ cups sugar
2 eggs
1 cup mashed ripe bananas
1 teaspoon vanilla
2¼ cups flour
1½ teaspoons baking powder
½ teaspoon soda
* * *
1 cup chopped pecans
2 tablespoons sugar
1 teaspoon cinnamon

Heat oven to 350°. Combine softened cream cheese, margarine and sugar, mixing until well blended. Add eggs, one at a time, mixing well after each addition. Blend in bananas and vanilla. Gradually add flour combined with baking powder and soda. Mix together nuts, sugar and cinnamon; fold half of nut mixture into batter. Pour into greased and floured 13 x 9-inch baking pan; sprinkle with remaining nut mixture. Bake at 350°, 35 to 40 minutes. 8 to 10 servings.

Apricot Crumble Cake

1 8-ounce package Philadelphia
Brand Cream Cheese
½ cup margarine
1¼ cups sugar
2 eggs
¼ cup milk
1 teaspoon vanilla
2 cups sifted cake flour
1 teaspoon baking powder
½ teaspoon soda
¼ teaspoon salt
1 10-ounce jar apricot or
peach preserves
* * *
2 cups shredded coconut
⅔ cup brown sugar, packed
1 teaspoon cinnamon
⅓ cup margarine, melted

Heat oven to 350°. Combine softened cream cheese, margarine and sugar, mixing until well blended. Add eggs, milk and vanilla; mix well. Add flour sifted with baking powder, soda and salt, mixing until well blended. Pour half of batter into greased and floured 13 x 9-inch baking pan. Cover with preserves; top with remaining batter. Bake at 350°, 35 to 40 minutes. Combine remaining ingredients; spread on cake. Broil until golden brown. 8 to 10 servings.

Opposite: Apricot Crumble Cake

"Philly" Apple Kuchen

2 cups biscuit mix
¼ cup sugar
2 tablespoons all purpose oil
1 egg
⅔ cup milk

* * *

1 8-ounce package Philadelphia
Brand Cream Cheese
¼ cup sugar
1 egg
¼ teaspoon vanilla

* * *

1½ cups sliced peeled apples
3 tablespoons sugar
¼ teaspoon cinnamon

Heat oven to 400°. Combine biscuit mix, ¼ cup sugar, oil, egg and milk; mix until well blended. Pour into greased 9-inch square pan. Combine softened cream cheese, ¼ cup sugar, egg and vanilla; mix until smooth. Pour cream cheese mixture over batter. Top with apple slices; sprinkle with combined sugar and cinnamon. Bake at 400°, 40 to 45 minutes. 8 to 10 servings.

Berry Patch Coffee Cake

1 8-ounce package Philadelphia
Brand Cream Cheese
½ cup margarine
1 cup sugar
2 eggs
½ teaspoon vanilla
2 cups sifted cake flour
1 teaspoon baking powder
½ teaspoon soda
¼ teaspoon salt
¼ cup milk
½ cup red raspberry preserves

Heat oven to 350°. Combine softened cream cheese, margarine and sugar, mixing until well blended. Add eggs, one at a time, mixing well after each addition. Blend in vanilla. Sift together dry ingredients; add alternately with milk, mixing well after each addition. Pour into greased and floured 13 x 9-inch baking pan; dot with preserves. Bake at 350°, 35 minutes. 8 to 10 servings.

Apple Cheddar Nut Bread

2½ cups flour
½ cup sugar
2 teaspoons baking powder
1 teaspoon salt
½ teaspoon cinnamon
¼ cup all purpose oil
2 eggs
¾ cup milk
1½ cups chopped peeled
apples
¾ cup chopped nuts
2 cups (8 ounces) shredded
Cracker Barrel Brand Sharp
Natural Cheddar Cheese

Heat oven to 350°. Combine flour, sugar, baking powder, salt and cinnamon. Add oil, eggs and milk; mix well. Stir in apples, nuts and cheese. Pour into well greased and floured 9 x 5-inch loaf pan. Bake at 350°, 1 hour and 15 minutes. Let stand 5 minutes; remove from pan. Cool.

Hearty Cheddar Biscuits

2 cups flour
1 tablespoon baking powder
1 teaspoon salt
¼ cup shortening
1½ cups (6 ounces) shredded
Cracker Barrel Brand Sharp
Natural Cheddar Cheese
½ cup chopped onion
2 tablespoons chopped
pimiento
¾ cup milk

Heat oven to 450°. Combine dry ingredients; cut in shortening. Add cheese, onion and pimiento. Add milk, stirring just until moistened. On lightly floured surface, roll dough to ½-inch thickness; cut with floured 3-inch cutter. Place on lightly greased baking sheet; bake at 450°, 15 minutes or until golden brown. 15 biscuits.

Cheddar Cornbread Ring

1 cup flour
1 cup yellow cornmeal
2 tablespoons sugar
1 tablespoon baking powder
1½ teaspoons salt
2 eggs, beaten
1 cup milk
2 cups (8 ounces) shredded
Cracker Barrel Brand Sharp
Natural Cheddar Cheese

Heat oven to 425°. Sift together dry ingredients. Add eggs, milk and cheese; stir until just blended. Pour into well greased, heated 1½-quart ring mold. Bake at 425°, 20 minutes. 6 servings.

Double Cheddar Cornbread

1 cup yellow cornmeal
1 cup flour
1 tablespoon baking powder
1 teaspoon salt
2 cups (8 ounces) shredded
Cracker Barrel Brand Sharp
Natural Cheddar Cheese
1 cup milk
¼ cup margarine, melted
1 egg, beaten
½ teaspoon dry mustard
4 slices crisply cooked
bacon, crumbled
1 green pepper, cut in rings

Heat oven to 425°. Sift together dry ingredients. Stir in 1 cup cheese. Combine milk, margarine and egg; add to dry ingredients, mixing until blended. Pour into greased 9-inch layer pan. Top with remaining cheese mixed with mustard. Sprinkle with bacon; top with green pepper rings. Bake at 425°, 25 minutes. 6 to 8 servings.

Parmesan Popovers

4 eggs
1 cup milk
⅔ cup flour
⅓ cup Kraft Grated
Parmesan Cheese
½ teaspoon salt

Heat oven to 450°. Preheat greased muffin pan or custard cups. Beat eggs; stir in milk. Add flour, cheese and salt; beat until well blended. Pour into muffin pan or cups. Bake at 450°, 15 minutes. Reduce temperature to 350°; continue baking 10 to 15 minutes or until golden. 12 to 15 large popovers.

Cheese Spoon Bread

1½ cups milk
¾ cup cornmeal
2 cups (8 ounces) shredded
Cracker Barrel Brand Sharp
Natural Cheddar Cheese
2 tablespoons margarine
½ teaspoon salt
Dash of cayenne
3 eggs, separated

Heat oven to 375°. Heat milk; stir in cornmeal until mixture is smooth and thickened. Remove from heat; blend in cheese, margarine, salt, cayenne and beaten egg yolks. Fold in stiffly beaten egg whites. Pour into greased 2-quart casserole. Bake at 375°, 40 to 45 minutes. 8 servings.

Cheese Bread

1 cup milk
2 tablespoons sugar
2 teaspoons salt
2 packages dry yeast
1½ cups warm water
5½ to 6 cups flour
2½ cups (10 ounces) shredded
Cracker Barrel Brand Sharp
Natural Cheddar Cheese
Margarine, melted

Scald milk; stir in sugar and salt. Cool to lukewarm. Dissolve yeast in water; add milk mixture. Stir in 4 cups flour; mix well. Add cheese and remaining flour, mixing until thoroughly blended. Knead until smooth and satiny on floured surface. Place dough in a greased bowl; brush with margarine. Cover; let rise in a warm place until double in bulk. Punch down; knead lightly. Divide dough in half; roll each half out to a rectangle. Roll up from short side; press ends to seal. Fold ends under loaf; place each loaf, seam side down, in greased 9 x 5-inch loaf pan. Brush with margarine. Cover; let rise until double in bulk. Heat oven to 375°; bake 50 minutes. Turn out of pan immediately. 2 loaves.

Cheddar Quick Bread

2 cups flour
1 tablespoon sugar
1½ teaspoons baking powder
½ teaspoon salt
¼ cup margarine
2 cups (8 ounces) shredded
Cracker Barrel Brand Sharp
Natural Cheddar Cheese
1 cup milk
1 egg, slightly beaten

Heat oven to 400°. Sift together dry ingredients. Cut in margarine until mixture resembles coarse crumbs; stir in cheese. Add milk and egg; mix just until moistened. Spoon into well greased 9 x 5-inch loaf pan; bake at 400°, 45 minutes.

Bohemian Cheese Bread

½ cup chopped onion
1 tablespoon margarine
1½ cups (6 ounces) shredded
Cracker Barrel Brand Sharp
Natural Cheddar Cheese
1 cup biscuit mix
⅓ cup milk
1 egg
1 tablespoon poppy seeds

Heat oven to 425°. Cook onion in margarine until tender. Combine ½ cup cheese and biscuit mix. Add milk; beat until dough is stiff. Knead on lightly floured board about 10 times. Pat

dough over bottom of 8-inch pie plate. Combine remaining cheese and egg; mix. Spread over biscuit dough; sprinkle with onion and poppy seeds. Bake at 425°, 20 minutes. Serve warm. 6 to 8 servings.

"Philly" Poppy Seed Bread

1 cup biscuit mix
⅓ cup milk
2 medium onions, sliced
2 tablespoons margarine
1 8-ounce package Philadelphia
Brand Cream Cheese
1 egg
½ teaspoon salt
1 teaspoon poppy seeds

Heat oven to 450°. Combine biscuit mix and milk; mix well. Spread into greased 9-inch square pan or pie plate. Cook onions in margarine until tender. Blend softened cream cheese, egg and salt; mix well. Combine cream cheese mixture and onions; spread over biscuit dough. Sprinkle with poppy seeds. Bake at 450°, 20 minutes. Serve warm. 8 servings.

Orange Crepes

3 eggs, beaten
⅔ cup flour
½ teaspoon salt
1 cup milk

* * *

1 8-ounce package Philadelphia
Brand Cream Cheese
¼ cup margarine
½ cup marshmallow creme
1 cup sifted confectioners'
sugar
¼ teaspoon almond extract
½ cup chopped almonds

* * *

1 10-ounce jar orange
marmalade
¼ cup Curaçao

Combine eggs, flour, salt and
milk; beat until smooth. Let
stand 30 minutes. For each
crepe, pour about 2 tablespoons batter into hot, lightly
greased skillet. Cook on one
side only. Combine softened
cream cheese and margarine;
mix until well blended. Stir in
marshmallow creme. Add sugar and almond extract; mix
well. Fold in almonds. Fill each
crepe with about ¼ cup of
cream cheese mixture. Place
crepes in chafing dish. Combine orange marmalade and
Curaçao; bring to a boil. Pour
over crepes. 8 servings.

Crepes Marquis

3 eggs, beaten
⅔ cup flour
½ teaspoon salt
1 cup milk

* * *

8 slices bacon
½ cup chopped onion
½ cup chopped green pepper
1 3-ounce can sliced
mushrooms, drained
2 cups (8 ounces) shredded
Cracker Barrel Brand Sharp
Natural Cheddar Cheese
1 8-ounce can tomato sauce

Combine eggs, flour, salt and
milk; beat until smooth. Let
stand 30 minutes. For each
crepe, pour ¼ cup batter into
hot, lightly greased skillet.
Cook on one side only. Heat
oven to 350°. Cook bacon until crisp; drain, reserving 2 tablespoons bacon fat. Crumble
bacon. Cook onion and green
pepper in bacon fat until tender.
Add bacon, mushrooms and
1½ cups cheese. Mix lightly.
Fill each crepe with about ¼
cup cheese mixture; roll. Place
crepes in 12 x 8-inch baking
dish; top with tomato sauce.
Bake at 350°, 15 minutes.
Sprinkle with remaining cheese;
return to oven until cheese
melts. 4 servings.

Red Raspberry Blintzes

⅔ cup milk
½ cup flour
2 eggs, beaten
1 tablespoon all purpose oil
1 tablespoon sugar
¼ teaspoon salt
Margarine
Kraft Whipped Cream Cheese
Red raspberry preserves

Combine milk, flour, eggs, oil, sugar and salt; mix until well blended. Batter should be very thin. For each blintz, pour ¼ cup batter into hot, lightly greased skillet; cook until lightly browned. Remove from skillet. Spread browned side with whipped cream cheese; roll up, folding sides toward center. Before serving, heat in margarine. Top with preserves. 6 blintzes.

Dutch Boy Pancake

4 cups sliced strawberries,
sliced peeled peaches or
blueberries
1 tablespoon Kirschwasser
*   *   *
2 cups (7-ounce jar) marsh-
mallow creme
1 8-ounce package Philadelphia
Brand Cream Cheese
*   *   *
½ cup milk
2 eggs
½ cup flour
¼ teaspoon salt
1 tablespoon margarine

Combine fruit and Kirschwasser; marinate ½ hour. Gradually add marshmallow creme to softened cream cheese, mixing until well blended. Heat oven to 450°. Combine milk, eggs, flour and salt; beat until smooth and well blended. Heat 9-inch skillet in oven until very hot. Add margarine to coat skillet; pour in batter immediately. Bake on lowest rack at 450°, 10 minutes. Reduce temperature to 350°; continue baking 10 minutes or until golden brown. Fill with fruit; top with cream cheese mixture. Serve immediately. 4 to 6 servings.

Another way: Omit first two ingredients. Heat 4 cups sliced peeled apples in ½ cup butterscotch topping. Spoon over pancake.

Crisp-fried Crullers

1 8-ounce package Philadelphia
Brand Cream Cheese
⅓ cup soft margarine
1 cup flour
Dash of salt
All purpose oil
Granulated sugar

Combine softened cream cheese and margarine; mix until well blended. Add flour and salt; mix thoroughly. Form into ball; chill 1 hour. On a floured surface, roll dough into a 12 x 6-inch rectangle. Cut dough into twenty-four ½-inch strips. Deep fry in hot oil, 400°, about 1 minute or until golden brown. Roll in sugar. 24 crullers.

Opposite: Dutch Boy Pancake

Cheese for Breakfast, Cheese for Brunch

Think about it for a moment: Cheese is a perfect accompaniment for such breakfast and brunch foods as eggs, bacon and breads of many kinds. Here are ways to add the flavor and nutrition of cheese to early-in-the-day meals.

Eggs Acapulco

½ pound Velveeta Pasteurized
Process Cheese Spread,
sliced
½ cup salad dressing
¼ cup milk
1 4½-ounce can shrimp,
drained
1 tablespoon chopped pimiento
4 hard-cooked eggs,
quartered
4 slices white bread,
toasted, cut in triangles

Combine Velveeta, salad dressing and milk; stir over low heat until sauce is smooth. Add shrimp and pimiento. Arrange eggs on toast; top with sauce. 4 servings.

Socialite's Brunch

2 tablespoons margarine
2 tablespoons flour
1 cup milk
¼ teaspoon salt
½ cup chopped cooked ham
1 3-ounce can sliced
mushrooms, drained
1 tablespoon sliced green onion
Kraft Natural Cheddar Cheese
Slices, cut in half
Sliced Italian bread, toasted

Make white sauce with margarine, flour, milk and salt. Stir in ham, mushrooms and onion; continue cooking 5 minutes. For each serving, place slices of cheese over toast; broil until cheese melts. Spoon sauce over cheese toast. 6 servings.

Eggs Royale

4 hard-cooked eggs
1 3-ounce can mushrooms,
drained, chopped
½ cup fresh bread crumbs
2 tablespoons margarine,
melted
Salt and pepper
½ pound Velveeta Pasteurized
Process Cheese Spread,
cubed
¼ cup milk
4 slices Canadian bacon,
cooked
4 slices white bread, toasted

Cut eggs in half lengthwise; remove yolks. Mash egg yolks; combine with mushrooms, bread crumbs and margarine. Season to taste. Spoon filling into egg white centers. Heat Velveeta with milk over low heat, stirring until sauce is smooth. For each serving, place slice of Canadian bacon on slice of toast; top with 2 egg halves and sauce. 4 servings.

Sunshine Sausageburgers

Ground sausage patties, cooked
English muffins, split,
toasted
Cracker Barrel Brand Sharp
Natural Cheddar Cheese,
sliced
Spiced apple rings

For each sandwich, place a sausage patty on half an English muffin. Top with 2 slices of cheese; broil until cheese melts. Top with an apple ring.

Western Eggs au Gratin

*½ pound Velveeta Pasteurized
Process Cheese Spread,
cubed
½ cup salad dressing
⅓ cup milk
1 5½-ounce jar boned
chicken, chopped or 1 cup
chopped cooked chicken
¼ cup sliced ripe olives
2 tablespoons chopped green
onion
4 hard-cooked eggs, quartered
4 English muffins, split,
toasted*

Combine Velveeta, salad dressing and milk; stir over low heat
until sauce is smooth. Add
chicken, olives and onion; heat.
Arrange eggs on muffins; top
with sauce. 4 servings.

Gourmet French Omelet

*1 2½-ounce jar mushrooms,
drained
3 tablespoons margarine
6 eggs, slightly beaten
⅓ cup milk
Salt and pepper
1 teaspoon finely chopped
chives
¾ cup (3 ounces) shredded
Cracker Barrel Brand Sharp
Natural Cheddar Cheese*

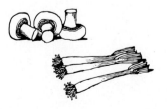

Cook mushrooms in 1 tablespoon margarine. Melt remaining margarine in skillet over low
heat. Combine eggs, milk and
seasonings; pour into skillet.
Cook slowly. As egg mixture
sets, lift slightly with a spatula
to allow uncooked portion to
flow underneath. Cover omelet with mushrooms, chives
and ½ cup cheese; fold in half
and sprinkle with remaining
cheese. 3 to 4 servings.

Country Breakfast

*4 cups cubed cooked
potatoes
½ cup chopped green pepper
2 tablespoons chopped onion
⅓ cup margarine
Salt and pepper
4 eggs
1 cup (4 ounces) shredded
Cracker Barrel Brand Sharp
Natural Cheddar Cheese*

Cook potatoes, green pepper
and onion in margarine until
lightly browned. Season to
taste. Break eggs over potato
mixture; cover and cook until
eggs are done. Sprinkle with
cheese; cover and heat until
cheese melts. 4 servings.

Opposite: Gourmet French Omelet

Sunny Scrambled Eggs

3 tablespoons margarine
¼ pound Velveeta Pasteurized
Process Cheese Spread,
cubed
6 eggs, beaten

Heat margarine in skillet. Add Velveeta to eggs; pour into skillet. Stir occasionally as eggs thicken. Cook until set. 4 servings.
Good idea: For children, serve scrambled eggs between toasted hamburger buns for a breakfast sandwich.

Biscayne Brunch

¼ cup milk
2 tablespoons margarine
1 8-ounce package
Philadelphia Brand Cream
Cheese, cubed
1 12-ounce package medium
shrimp, cooked
1 6-ounce can water
chestnuts, drained,
sliced
½ cup peas, cooked
¼ cup finely chopped onion
¼ cup dry white wine
2 tablespoons chopped
parsley
2 tablespoons chopped
pimiento
¼ teaspoon salt
Dash of pepper
*   *   *   *
6 patty shells

Heat milk, margarine and cream cheese over low heat; stir until smooth. Stir in remaining ingredients; heat thoroughly. Serve in patty shells. 6 servings.

Swiss Omelet Puff

6 eggs, separated
2 tablespoons chopped
parsley
2 tablespoons milk
½ teaspoon salt
1 6-ounce package Kraft
Natural Swiss Cheese
Slices, cut in thin
strips
4 slices crisply cooked
bacon, crumbled

Heat oven to 325°. Combine egg yolks, parsley, milk and salt; beat until thick and lemon colored. Add two-thirds of cheese. Fold in stiffly beaten egg whites. Pour into sizzling, well greased 10-inch skillet. Cook over low heat 10 minutes or until underside is golden brown. Bake at 325°, 10 to 15 minutes or until top is firm. Remove from oven; make deep crease across top. Place bacon and remaining cheese on half of omelet. Slip turner underneath, tip skillet to loosen and gently fold in half. 6 servings.

Denver Omelet

¼ cup chopped green pepper
1 tablespoon chopped onion
¼ cup margarine
6 eggs, slightly beaten
½ cup chopped cooked ham
⅓ cup milk
Salt and pepper

*4 Old English Sharp
Pasteurized Process
American Cheese Slices*

Cook green pepper and onion in 2 tablespoons margarine until tender; add remaining 2 tablespoons of margarine. Combine eggs, ham, milk and seasonings; pour into skillet. Cook slowly. As egg mixture sets, lift slightly with spatula to allow uncooked portion to flow underneath. Place 2 slices of cheese on one half of omelet; fold in half. Top with remaining cheese slices. 3 to 4 servings.

Spanish Potato Omelet

*2 tablespoons margarine
1½ cups diced potatoes
½ cup chopped green pepper
⅓ cup chopped onion
¼ cup chopped pimiento
½ teaspoon salt
8 eggs
½ teaspoon salt
* * *
Dash of pepper
Kraft Natural Swiss Cheese
Slices, cut in
triangles*

Heat oven to 350°. Heat margarine in skillet; add potatoes, green pepper and onion. Cover; cook 10 minutes or until tender, stirring occasionally. Stir in pimiento and salt. Spoon into well greased 10 x 6-inch baking dish. Beat eggs with seasonings; pour over vegetables. Bake at 350°, 20 to 25 minutes or until eggs

are set. Top with cheese; continue baking until cheese melts. 8 servings.

Eggs El Dorado

*¼ cup chopped onion
¼ cup chopped green pepper
2 tablespoons margarine
1 8-ounce jar Cheez Whiz
Pasteurized Process Cheese
Spread
4 hard-cooked eggs, sliced
2 tablespoons chopped
pimiento
4 English muffins, split,
toasted*

Cook onion and green pepper in margarine until tender. Add Cheez Whiz, eggs and pimiento; heat. For each serving, spoon mixture over 2 muffin halves. 4 servings.

Savory Scrambled Eggs

*2 tablespoons margarine
6 eggs, beaten
⅓ cup milk
Salt and pepper
1 3-ounce package
Philadelphia Brand Cream
Cheese, cubed*

Melt margarine in skillet over low heat; add combined eggs, milk and seasonings. Cook slowly, stirring until eggs begin to thicken. Add cream cheese; continue cooking, stirring occasionally, until cheese is melted and eggs are cooked. 4 to 6 servings.

Bacon 'n Eggs—Pizza Style

1 can (8 ounces)
refrigerated flaky
buttermilk biscuits
3 eggs, beaten
1 tablespoon milk
Dash of salt
5 slices crisply cooked
bacon, crumbled
1 teaspoon chopped chives
1 cup (4 ounces) shredded
Cracker Barrel Brand Sharp
Natural Cheddar Cheese

Press the flat sides of 2 biscuits together. On a baking sheet, flatten into 5-inch circles, building rims around each; refrigerate. Heat oven to 350°. Combine eggs, milk and salt. Pour into biscuit shells. Sprinkle with bacon, chives and cheese. Bake at 350°, 20 minutes. Top with additional slices of crisply cooked bacon, if desired. 5 servings.

Golden Omelet

2 tablespoons margarine
6 eggs, beaten
¼ cup milk
¼ teaspoon salt
Dash of pepper
¼ pound Velveeta
Pasteurized Process
Cheese Spread, sliced

Melt margarine in skillet over low heat. Combine eggs, milk and seasonings; pour into skillet. Cook slowly. As egg mixture sets, lift slightly with a spatula to allow uncooked portion to flow underneath. Place 3 slices of Velveeta on omelet; fold in half. Remove from skillet; top with remaining Velveeta. 3 to 4 servings.

Cheesy Apple Tarts

1 can (8.6 ounces)
refrigerated butterflake
dinner rolls
3 apples, cored and cut into
¼-inch wedges
Margarine
1½ cups (6 ounces) shredded
Cracker Barrel Brand Sharp
Natural Cheddar Cheese
Apple jelly or raspberry
preserves

Press the flat sides of 2 rolls together. On a baking sheet, flatten into circles, building rims around each; refrigerate. Heat oven to 375°. Cook apples in small amount of margarine 3 to 5 minutes or until slightly tender. Place apple slices in roll shells. Bake at 375°, 10 minutes. Sprinkle with cheese and return to oven for 5 more minutes. Top each with 1 teaspoon jelly or preserves, if desired. 6 servings.

Beautiful Salads, Tasty Dressings

Something fresh. Something green, something crunchy, with
cheese to make it doubly good. Here are such salads—
and main dish salads as well—plus a bonus of
taste-like-more dressings that will be family favorites.

Pimiento Dressing

1 5-ounce jar Kraft
Pimento Pasteurized
Neufchatel Cheese Spread
¼ cup milk

Combine cheese spread and milk; mix well. Serve on vegetable salads. ¾ cup.

"Philly" Orange Dressing

1 8-ounce package Philadelphia
Brand Cream Cheese
¼ cup orange juice
1 tablespoon sugar
1 tablespoon grated orange rind

Combine softened cream cheese and remaining ingredients, mixing until well blended. 1¼ cups.
Another way: Substitute 2 tablespoons chopped maraschino cherries for grated orange rind.

Prima Donna Dressing

1 5-ounce jar Kraft
Pineapple Pasteurized
Neufchatel Cheese Spread
½ cup heavy cream, whipped
2 tablespoons chopped nuts

Combine cheese spread and whipped cream; mix until well blended. Stir in nuts. Serve on fruit salad. 1⅔ cups.

Jubilee Salad Bowl

Cracker Barrel Brand Sharp
Stixpak
Head lettuce
6 boiled ham slices, cut
in strips
1 cup orange sections
1 apple, thinly sliced
½ cup green grapes, cut
in half
Spicy sweet French dressing

Cut two 2-ounce sticks of cheese in strips. Cut lettuce in 2-inch chunks into salad bowl. Add cheese, ham, fruit and enough dressing to moisten. 4 to 6 servings.

"Philly" Fruit Salad

3 tablespoons milk
1 8-ounce package Philadelphia
Brand Cream Cheese
1 8-ounce can mandarin
orange sections, drained
1 13½-ounce can crushed
pineapple, drained
1 8¾-ounce can seedless
grapes, drained
10 maraschino cherries, halved
½ cup coconut, toasted

Gradually add milk to softened cream cheese, mixing until well blended. Add remaining ingredients; mix well. Chill several hours or overnight. 6 servings.

Heavenly Cheese Mold

*1¼ cups (13½-ounce can)
crushed pineapple
1 3-ounce package lemon
flavored gelatin
1 cup boiling water
1 tablespoon lemon juice
1 cup (4 ounces) shredded
Cracker Barrel Brand Sharp
Natural Cheddar Cheese
1 cup heavy cream, whipped*

Drain pineapple, reserving syrup. Add enough water to syrup to make ¾ cup liquid. Dissolve gelatin in boiling water; add syrup and lemon juice. Chill until slightly thickened. Fold in pineapple, cheese and whipped cream; pour into 1½-quart mold. Chill until firm; unmold. 6 to 8 servings.

"Philly" Frozen Party Salad

*¼ cup honey
1 8-ounce package Philadelphia
Brand Cream Cheese
2 10-ounce packages frozen
raspberries, thawed
1 cup heavy cream, whipped*

Gradually add honey to softened cream cheese, mixing until well blended. Stir in raspberries. Fold in whipped cream. Pour into 9-inch square pan or eight ¾-cup molds; freeze until firm. 8 servings.

Top-Notch Turkey Mold

*1 envelope unflavored
gelatin
¾ cup cold water
1 10-ounce package frozen
cranberry-orange relish,
thawed
* * **

*1 envelope unflavored gelatin
¾ cup cold water
1 8-ounce package Philadelphia
Brand Cream Cheese
1 cup salad dressing
1½ cups diced cooked turkey
⅓ cup sliced celery
¼ cup chopped walnuts*

Soften gelatin in cold water; stir over low heat until dissolved. Chill until slightly thickened. Stir in relish. Pour into 1½-quart ring mold; chill until firm. Soften gelatin in cold water; stir over low heat until dissolved. Combine softened cream cheese and salad dressing. Gradually add gelatin to cream cheese mixture, mixing until well blended. Chill until slightly thickened; fold in turkey, celery and nuts. Pour over molded gelatin layer; chill until firm. Unmold. 6 to 8 servings.

Imperial Peach Salad

1 1-pound can sliced peaches
1 3-ounce package cherry
flavored gelatin
1 cup boiling water
* * *
1 3-ounce package cherry
flavored gelatin
1 cup boiling water
¾ cup cold water
1 8-ounce package Philadelphia
Brand Cream Cheese

Drain peaches, reserving 1 cup syrup. Dissolve gelatin in boiling water; add syrup. Chill until slightly thickened. Arrange peach slices in bottom of 1½-quart ring mold; cover with gelatin. Chill until firm. Dissolve gelatin in boiling water; add cold water. Gradually add to softened cream cheese, mixing until well blended. Pour over molded gelatin layer; chill until firm. Unmold. 8 to 10 servings.

Creamy Orange Salad

1 3-ounce package orange
flavored gelatin
1½ cups boiling water
1 8-ounce package Philadelphia
Brand Cream Cheese
¼ cup orange juice
1 tablespoon lemon juice
1 tablespoon grated orange rind
Lettuce

Dissolve gelatin in boiling water. Gradually add to softened cream cheese, mixing until well blended. Stir in juices and orange rind. Pour into 1-quart mold; chill until firm. Unmold; surround with lettuce. 4 to 6 servings.

Emerald Isle Mold

1 3-ounce package lime
flavored gelatin
1 cup boiling water
¾ cup cold water
1 8-ounce package Philadelphia
Brand Cream Cheese
* * *
1 3-ounce package lime
flavored gelatin
1 cup boiling water
1 cup ginger ale
1 cup grapefruit sections,
cut in half
1 cup diced apples
¼ cup chopped walnuts

Dissolve gelatin in boiling water; add cold water. Gradually add to softened cream cheese, mixing until well blended. Pour into 1½-quart mold; chill until firm. Dissolve gelatin in boiling water; add ginger ale. Chill until slightly thickened; fold in fruit and nuts. Pour over molded gelatin layer; chill until firm. Unmold. 6 to 8 servings.

Hawaiian Supper Salad

1 7-ounce package elbow
macaroni, cooked, drained
1⅓ cups (13½-ounce can)
pineapple tidbits, drained
1 cup (4 ounces) shredded
Cracker Barrel Brand Sharp
Natural Cheddar Cheese
1 cup cooked ham strips
⅓ cup chopped green pepper
¼ cup chopped sweet pickles
1 tablespoon chopped onion
¼ teaspoon salt
Dash of pepper
Salad dressing

Combine macaroni, pineapple, cheese, ham, green pepper, pickles, onion, seasonings and enough salad dressing to moisten; toss lightly. Chill. 8 servings.

Aristocrat's Antipasto

Unpeeled cucumber, thinly
sliced
Pitted ripe olives
Sliced mushrooms
Italian-style dressing
Cherry peppers
Kraft Natural Swiss Cheese
Slices, cut in strips

Marinate cucumber, olives and mushrooms in dressing for several hours; drain. Arrange marinated vegetables on platter with cherry peppers and cheese strips.

Party Chicken Salad

½ pound Tasty Brand Imitation
Pasteurized Process Cheese
Spread, cubed
2 cups cubed cooked chicken
1 cup drained pineapple tidbits
1 cup sliced celery
1 cup seeded halved green
grapes
Salad dressing
Lettuce

Combine Tasty Brand, chicken, pineapple, celery, grapes and enough salad dressing to moisten; toss lightly. Serve in lettuce-lined salad bowl. 6 servings.

Gold Rush Salad

1 8-ounce package Kraft
Pasteurized Process American
Cheese Slices
2 cups (1-pound can) kidney
beans, drained
1 cup sliced celery
⅓ cup chopped green pepper
¼ cup chopped onion
3 hard-cooked eggs, chopped
Dash of pepper
Pourable Thousand Island
dressing
Lettuce

Cut 5 slices of cheese in small squares. Combine cheese, beans, celery, green pepper, onion, eggs, pepper and enough dressing to moisten; toss lightly. Chill. Cut remaining cheese in triangles. Serve salad on lettuce; top with cheese triangles. 6 servings.

Fiesta Bean Salad

*2 cups (1-pound can) kidney
beans, drained
½ pound Velveeta Pasteurized
Process Cheese Spread,
cut in strips
3 hard-cooked eggs, sliced
1 cup sliced celery
½ cup onion rings
½ cup pourable Thousand
Island dressing
1 teaspoon salt
Dash of pepper*

Combine all ingredients; toss
lightly. Chill. 6 to 8 servings.

Wilted Spinach Bowl

*4 slices bacon
2 tablespoons vinegar
2 tablespoons finely chopped
onion
¼ teaspoon pepper
6 cups fresh spinach
½ cup Kraft Grated
Parmesan Cheese
1 hard-cooked egg, chopped*

Cook bacon until crisp; drain,
reserving ¼ cup bacon fat. Add
vinegar, onion and pepper to
bacon fat; heat. Tear spinach
into bite-size pieces into a salad
bowl. Crumble bacon; toss
with spinach and cheese in
dressing until well coated; top
with egg. 6 servings.

Mariner's Macaroni Salad

*1 7-ounce package elbow maca-
roni, cooked, drained
1 12-ounce can luncheon meat,
cubed
¾ cup sliced celery
⅓ cup chopped onion
¼ cup chopped green pepper
¼ cup chopped pimiento
¼ cup Kraft Grated
Parmesan Cheese
Dash of pepper
Mayonnaise*

Combine all ingredients except
mayonnaise; toss. Add enough
mayonnaise to moisten; mix
well. Chill. 4 to 5 servings.

Piccadilly Salad

*1 8-ounce jar Cheez Whiz
Pasteurized Process
Cheese Spread
¼ cup milk
1 7-ounce package elbow
macaroni, cooked, drained
½ cup sliced sweet pickles
¼ cup chopped onion
¼ cup chopped celery
2 tablespoons chopped
pimiento
6 hard-cooked eggs, chopped*

Heat Cheez Whiz with milk in
saucepan over low heat; stir until sauce is smooth. Add remaining ingredients; mix well. Heat.
6 servings.

Monterey Macaroni Salad

1 7-ounce package elbow
macaroni, cooked, drained
1 8-ounce jar Cheez Whiz
Pasteurized Process
Cheese Spread
¼ cup salad dressing
½ teaspoon salt
Dash of pepper
¾ cup sliced celery
½ cup diced salami
¼ cup sliced radishes

Combine hot macaroni, Cheez Whiz, salad dressing and seasonings. Add remaining ingredients; mix well. Chill. 4 to 6 servings.

Sunbonnet Macaroni Salad

1 7-ounce package elbow
macaroni, cooked, drained
1 8-ounce jar Cheez Whiz
Pasteurized Process
Cheese Spread
8 slices crisply cooked bacon,
crumbled
¼ cup chopped green pepper
1 tablespoon chopped onion

Combine hot macaroni and Cheez Whiz; mix well. Add remaining ingredients; mix well. Chill. 4 to 6 servings.
Nice to know: This salad may also be served hot.

Potato Salad Parmigiana

¾ cup sliced celery
½ cup chopped green pepper
⅓ cup chopped onion
⅔ cup Italian-style dressing
6 cups sliced cooked potatoes
4 hard-cooked eggs, chopped
6 slices crisply cooked
bacon, crumbled
¾ cup (3 ounces) Kraft
Grated Parmesan Cheese

Cook celery, green pepper and onion in dressing 5 minutes. Add potatoes, eggs, bacon and cheese; mix lightly. Heat, stirring occasionally. Top with additional cheese, if desired. 6 to 8 servings.

Cheddar Potato Salad

4 cups diced cooked potatoes
1 10-ounce stick Cracker
Barrel Brand Sharp Natural
Cheddar Cheese, cubed
1 cup sliced celery
1 cup thinly sliced carrots
3 hard-cooked eggs, chopped
¼ cup chopped green onion
1 cup salad dressing
1 tablespoon prepared mustard
1½ teaspoons salt
Dash of pepper

Combine ingredients; toss lightly. Chill. 6 to 8 servings.

Parmesan Potato Salad

4 cups diced cooked potatoes
4 hard-cooked eggs, chopped
1 cup sliced celery
¼ cup chopped onion
¼ cup chopped green pepper
1 teaspoon salt
8 slices crisply cooked
bacon, crumbled
¾ cup Kraft Grated
Parmesan Cheese
Salad dressing

Combine potatoes, eggs, celery, onion, green pepper, salt, bacon, cheese and enough salad dressing to moisten; mix lightly. Chill. Sprinkle with additional cheese, if desired. 6 to 8 servings.

Sunny Potato Salad

6 slices bacon
6 cups sliced cooked potatoes
½ cup chopped onion
½ cup chopped green pepper
½ cup sliced celery
2 teaspoons salt
Dash of pepper
1 cup (4 ounces) shredded
Cracker Barrel Brand Sharp
Natural Cheddar Cheese

Cook bacon in skillet; crumble. Add remaining ingredients except cheese; mix lightly. Cover; cook 15 minutes. Sprinkle with cheese; cover until cheese melts. 6 servings.

Mexican Salad

1 pound ground beef
¼ cup chopped onion
2 cups (1-pound can) kidney
beans, drained
½ cup spicy sweet French
dressing
½ cup water
1 tablespoon chili powder
*   *   *
4 cups shredded lettuce
½ cup sliced green onions
2 cups (8 ounces) shredded
Cracker Barrel Brand Sharp
Natural Cheddar Cheese

Brown meat; drain. Add onion and cook until tender. Stir in beans, dressing, water and chili powder; simmer 15 minutes. Combine lettuce and green onions. Add meat sauce and 1½ cups cheese; toss lightly. Sprinkle with remaining cheese. Serve with crisp tortillas, if desired. 4 to 6 servings.

Starboard Bean Salad

2 cups (1-pound can) cut
green beans, drained
2 cups (1-pound can) lima
beans, drained
2 cups (1-pound can) kidney
beans, drained
½ cup diced tomato
¼ cup chopped celery
2 cups (8 ounces) cubed
Cracker Barrel Brand Sharp
Natural Cheddar Cheese
Spicy sweet French dressing

Combine vegetables and cheese with enough dressing to moisten. Chill. 10 to 12 servings.

Soufflés and Fondues, Sweet and Savory

Cheese soufflés light as clouds, cheese fondues rich
and delicious—these are dishes that parties can center
around, that make everyone feel this must be a special
occasion when they put in an appearance at a family meal.

Parmesan Cheese Soufflé

3 tablespoons margarine
3 tablespoons flour
1¼ cups milk
½ teaspoon salt
Dash of pepper
½ cup Kraft Grated Parmesan
Cheese
1 cup (4 ounces) shredded
Cracker Barrel Brand Sharp
Natural Cheddar Cheese
4 eggs, separated

Heat oven to 350°. Make white sauce with margarine, flour, milk and seasonings. Add Parmesan cheese and Cheddar cheese; stir until melted. Remove from heat. Gradually add slightly beaten egg yolks; cool. Fold into stiffly beaten egg whites. Pour into 1½-quart soufflé dish. With tip of spoon, make slight indentation or "track" around top of soufflé 1 inch in from edge to form a top hat. Bake at 350°, 45 to 50 minutes. Serve immediately. 6 servings.

Georgian Spinach Soufflé

¼ cup margarine
¼ cup flour
¾ cup milk
½ pound Velveeta Pasteurized
Process Cheese
Spread, cubed
¼ teaspoon pepper
1 10-ounce package frozen
chopped spinach, cooked,
drained
6 slices crisply cooked bacon,
crumbled
1 tablespoon finely chopped
onion
4 eggs, separated

Heat oven to 350°. Make white sauce with margarine, flour and milk. Add Velveeta and pepper; stir until melted. Remove from heat; stir in spinach, bacon and onion. Gradually add slightly beaten egg yolks; cool slightly. Fold in stiffly beaten egg whites; pour into 1½-quart soufflé dish. Bake at 350°, 45 minutes. 8 servings.

Crabmeat Soufflé

1½ cups (6½-ounce can)
crabmeat, drained, flaked
¼ cup margarine
¼ cup flour
1 cup milk
½ teaspoon salt
1 cup (4 ounces) shredded
Cracker Barrel Brand Sharp
Natural Cheddar Cheese
4 eggs, separated

Heat oven to 300°. Place crabmeat in bottom of 5-cup soufflé dish. Make white sauce with margarine, flour, milk and salt. Add cheese; stir until melted. Remove from heat. Add slightly beaten egg yolks; cool. Fold into stiffly beaten egg whites; pour over crabmeat in soufflé dish. With tip of spoon, make slight indentation or "track" around top of soufflé 1-inch in from edge to form a top hat. Bake at 300°, 1 hour to 1 hour and 5 minutes. Serve immediately. 4 servings.

Top Hat Cheese Soufflé

⅓ cup margarine
⅓ cup flour
1½ cups milk
1 teaspoon salt
Dash of cayenne
2 cups (8 ounces) shredded
Cracker Barrel Brand Sharp
Natural Cheddar Cheese
6 eggs, separated

Heat oven to 300°. Make white sauce with margarine, flour, milk and seasonings. Add cheese; stir until melted. Remove from heat. Gradually add slightly beaten egg yolks; cool. Fold into stiffly beaten egg whites; pour into 2-quart soufflé dish or casserole. With tip of spoon, make slight indentation or "track" around top of soufflé 1-inch in from edge to form a top hat. Bake at 300°, 1 hour and 15 minutes. Serve immediately. 6 servings.

Another way: For individual soufflés, pour mixture into 6 individual soufflé dishes. Bake at 300°, 45 minutes.

Chocolate "Philly" Soufflé

2 tablespoons margarine
2 tablespoons flour
1 cup milk
¼ teaspoon salt
*1 8-ounce package Philadelphia
Brand Cream Cheese, cubed*
*2 1-ounce squares unsweetened
chocolate, melted*
1½ teaspoons vanilla
4 eggs, separated
⅔ cup sugar

Heat oven to 350°. Make white
sauce with margarine, flour,
milk and salt. Add cream cheese,
chocolate and vanilla; stir until cheese is melted. Remove
from heat. Beat egg yolks until
thick and lemon colored; gradually add sugar. Stir into cream
cheese mixture; cool slightly.
Fold into stiffly beaten egg
whites; pour into 2-quart soufflé dish. With tip of spoon,
make slight indentation or
"track" around top of soufflé 1
inch in from edge to form top
hat. Bake at 350°, 45 minutes.
6 servings.

Grasshopper Soufflé

2 envelopes unflavored gelatin
2 cups water
1 cup sugar
4 eggs, separated
*1 8-ounce package Philadelphia
Brand Cream Cheese*
¼ cup crème de menthe
1 cup heavy cream, whipped

Soften gelatin in ½ cup water;
add remaining water. Stir over
low heat until dissolved. Remove from heat; blend in ¾
cup sugar and beaten egg yolks.
Return to heat; cook 2 to 3 minutes. Gradually add to softened
cream cheese, mixing until well
blended. Stir in crème de
menthe; chill until slightly
thickened. Beat egg whites until soft peaks form. Gradually
add remaining sugar, beating
until stiff peaks form. Fold egg
whites and whipped cream into
cream cheese mixture. Wrap a
3-inch collar of aluminum foil
around top of 1½-quart soufflé
dish; secure with tape. Pour
mixture into dish; chill until
firm. Remove foil collar before
serving. Garnish with additional whipped cream and strawberries, if desired. 8 to 10 servings.

Heavenly Cream Soufflé

2 envelopes unflavored gelatin
2 cups water
1 cup sugar
4 eggs, separated
*1 8-ounce package Philadelphia
Brand Cream Cheese*
¼ cup crème de cacao
1 cup heavy cream, whipped
Peach Sauce

Soften gelatin in ½ cup water;
gradually add remaining water.
Stir over low heat until dissolved. Remove from heat;
blend in ¾ cup sugar and beat-
en egg yolks. Return to heat;
cook 2 to 3 minutes. Gradually

add to softened cream cheese, mixing until well blended. Stir in crème de cacao; chill until slightly thickened. Beat egg whites until soft peaks form. Gradually add remaining sugar, beating until stiff peaks form. Fold egg whites and whipped cream into cream cheese mixture. Wrap a 3-inch collar of aluminum foil around top of 1½-quart soufflé dish; secure with tape. Pour mixture into dish; chill until firm. Remove foil collar before serving. Serve with Peach Sauce. 8 to 10 servings.

Peach Sauce

2 10-ounce packages frozen peaches, thawed
1 tablespoon cornstarch

Drain peaches, reserving juice. Combine juice and cornstarch in saucepan. Bring to a boil, stirring constantly. Continue cooking until clear and thickened. Stir in peaches; cool. 2 cups.

New Orleans Chocolate Soufflé

2 envelopes unflavored gelatin
2¼ cups water
1½ cups sugar
3 1-ounce squares unsweetened chocolate
4 eggs, separated
1 8-ounce package Philadelphia Brand Cream Cheese
2 teaspoons grated orange rind
1 cup heavy cream, whipped

Soften gelatin in ½ cup water; stir over low heat until dissolved. Combine 1 cup sugar, chocolate, beaten egg yolks and remaining 1¾ cups water; stir over medium heat until chocolate is melted. Gradually add chocolate mixture and gelatin to softened cream cheese, mixing until well blended. Stir in orange rind. Chill until slightly thickened. Beat egg whites until soft peaks form. Gradually add remaining sugar and beat until stiff peaks form. Fold egg whites and whipped cream into chocolate mixture. Wrap a 3-inch collar of aluminum foil around top of 1½-quart soufflé dish; secure with tape. Pour mixture into dish; chill until firm. Remove foil collar before serving. 8 to 10 servings.
Another way: Omit orange rind. Add ½ teaspoon almond extract.

157

High Rise Strawberry Soufflés

2 envelopes unflavored gelatin
2¼ cups water
1 10-ounce package frozen
    strawberries, thawed
1 8-ounce package Philadelphia
    Brand Cream Cheese
⅔ cup sugar
1 tablespoon lemon juice
1 cup heavy cream, whipped
Red food coloring

Soften gelatin in ½ cup water; add remaining water. Stir over low heat until dissolved. Drain strawberries, reserving juice. Combine softened cream cheese and sugar, mixing until well blended. Gradually add gelatin, lemon juice and juice from strawberries; mix well. Chill until slightly thickened. Fold in strawberries, whipped cream and a few drops of food coloring. Wrap 3-inch collars of aluminum foil around individual dessert dishes or cups; secure with tape. Pour mixture into dishes; chill until firm. Remove foil collars before serving. 8 to 10 servings.

Another way: A 1½-quart soufflé dish may be used.

Swiss Cheese Fondue

1 8-ounce package Kraft
    Natural Swiss Cheese Slices,
    cut in strips
1 tablespoon flour
1 garlic clove, cut in half
1 cup dry white wine
Salt and pepper
Dash of nutmeg
2 tablespoons Kirschwasser
French or Vienna bread, cut
    in chunks

Toss together cheese and flour. Rub inside of fondue cooker, chafing dish or electric skillet with garlic. Pour in wine; heat until bubbles rise to surface. (Never let it boil.) Add cheese mixture, ½ cup at a time. Stir constantly, letting each amount melt completely before adding more. Continue stirring until mixture bubbles lightly. Stir in seasonings and Kirschwasser. Keep fondue bubbling while serving. Dip chunks of bread into fondue. If fondue becomes too thick, pour in a little warmed wine. 3 to 4 servings.

Zippy Fondue

¼ cup margarine
¼ cup flour
2 cups milk
½ teaspoon salt
Dash of pepper
2½ cups (10 ounces) shredded
    Cracker Barrel Brand Sharp
    Natural Cheddar Cheese
¼ cup sliced green onion
French or rye bread, cut in
    chunks

Make white sauce with margarine, flour, milk and seasonings. Add cheese and onion; stir until cheese is melted. Pour into fondue dish. Dip chunks of bread in fondue mixture. 3½ cups.

Crowd-Pleasing Fondue

1 5-ounce jar Kraft Olive-
Pimento Pasteurized
Neufchatel Cheese Spread
1 5-ounce jar Old English
Sharp Pasteurized Process
Cheese Spread
1 tablespoon water
Corn chips
French bread, cut in chunks

Heat cheese spreads and water over low heat, stirring until smooth. Pour into fondue dish. Dip corn chips or bread chunks in mixture. 1 cup.

Hearty "Philly" Fondue

1 2¼-ounce jar sliced dried
beef
1¾ cups milk
2 8-ounce packages
Philadelphia Brand Cream
Cheese, cubed
¼ cup chopped green onion
2 teaspoons dry mustard
French bread, cut in chunks

Rinse dried beef in hot water; drain and chop. Heat milk and cream cheese over low heat; stir until cream cheese is melted. Add dried beef, onion and mustard to cream cheese mixture. Cook 5 minutes over low heat. Pour into fondue dish. Dip chunks of bread in fondue mixture. 10 to 12 servings.

Fontainebleau Fondue

1 8-ounce package Philadelphia
Brand Cream Cheese, cubed
½ cup milk
⅔ cup sugar
2 1-ounce squares unsweetened
chocolate
1 tablespoon brandy
Pound cake, cubed
Miniature marshmallows
Strawberries
Bananas, sliced

Heat cream cheese and milk in saucepan over low heat, stirring until well blended. Add sugar and chocolate. Heat until mixture is smooth, sitrring constantly. Add brandy; pour into fondue dish. Dip pound cake, marshmallows, strawberries or banana slices in fondue mixture. 6 to 8 servings.

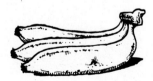

Cheese Cakes and Pies, Pastries and Other Sweets

Here are desserts to bring every meal—from the simplest family dinner to the most elaborate company-coming occasion—to a happy ending; cheese stars in all these recipes, making each dish something very special indeed.

Princess Brownies

1 package family-size brownie
mix
1 8-ounce package Philadelphia
Brand Cream Cheese
⅓ cup sugar
½ teaspoon vanilla
1 egg

Heat oven to 350°. Prepare brownie mix as directed on package. Combine softened cream cheese and sugar; mix until well blended. Stir in vanilla and egg. Spread half of brownie batter into greased 13 x 9-inch baking pan; cover with cream cheese mixture and spoon on remaining brownie batter. Bake at 350°, 35 to 40 minutes. Cool. Cut in 1½-inch squares. 4 dozen.
Nice to know: This recipe may be doubled.

Fruit 'n Cheese Bars

2¾ cups flour
1 teaspoon baking powder
½ teaspoon salt
¾ cup margarine
2½ cups (10 ounces) shredded
Cracker Barrel Brand Sharp
Natural Cheddar Cheese
2 eggs, beaten
½ cup peach preserves
½ cup strawberry preserves

Heat oven to 350°. Sift together dry ingredients. Cut in margarine until pieces are size of peas. Add cheese; toss lightly. Add eggs; mix well. Chill one quar- ter of dough. Press remaining dough onto bottom and sides of ungreased 15½ x 10½-inch jelly roll pan. Spread half of dough with peach preserves and remaining half with straw- berry preserves. Roll chilled dough on lightly floured sur- face; cut into ½-inch strips. Place strips diagonally across preserves to form lattice; press around edges to seal. Bake at 350°, 35 minutes or until lightly browned. Cool before cutting into 2 x 3-inch bars. 2 dozen.

"Philly" Chippers

1 cup margarine
1 8-ounce package Philadelphia
Brand Cream Cheese
¾ cup sugar
¾ cup brown sugar, packed
1 egg
1 teaspoon vanilla
2½ cups flour
1 teaspoon baking powder
½ teaspoon salt
1 12-ounce package semi-sweet
chocolate pieces
½ cup chopped nuts

Heat oven to 375°. Combine margarine, softened cream cheese and sugar; mix well. Stir in egg and vanilla. Add combined flour, baking powder and salt; mix well. Stir in choc- olate pieces and nuts. Drop by teaspoonfuls onto greased bak- ing sheet. Bake at 375°, 15 to 18 minutes. 5½ dozen.

Holiday Gift Cake

1 8-ounce package Philadelphia
Brand Cream Cheese
1 cup margarine
1½ cups sugar
1½ teaspoons vanilla
4 eggs
2¼ cups sifted cake flour
1½ teaspoons baking powder
¾ cup (8-ounce jar) well-
drained chopped maraschino
cherries
½ cup chopped pecans
*   *   *
½ cup finely chopped pecans
Maraschino cherries
Pecans

Heat oven to 325°. Thoroughly blend softened cream cheese, margarine, sugar and vanilla. Add eggs, one at a time, mixing well after each addition. Gradually add 2 cups flour sifted with baking powder. Combine remaining flour with cherries and ½ cup nuts; fold into batter. Grease 10-inch bundt or tube pan; sprinkle with ½ cup finely chopped nuts. Pour batter into pan; bake at 325°, 1 hour and 20 minutes. Cool 5 minutes; remove from pan. Glaze with mixture of 1½ cups sifted confectioners' sugar and 2 tablespoons milk. Garnish with cherries and pecans. 18 to 20 servings.

Nice to know: These cakes make excellent gifts. Bake the cakes in cans or other containers, as suggested below, and omit the ½ cup finely chopped nuts for lining pans.

1. Pour 2 cups batter into each of three greased 1-pound coffee cans. Bake at 325°, 1 hour.
2. Pour 1½ cups batter into each of four greased 1-pound shortening cans. Bake at 325°, 1 hour.
3. Pour ½ cup batter into each of eleven greased 8-ounce tomato sauce cans. Bake at 325°, 25 minutes.
4. Pour 1 cup batter into each of five greased 6 x 3½-inch loaf pans. Bake at 325°, 45 to 50 minutes.

Choco-Cherry Cookies

1 cup margarine
1 8-ounce package Philadelphia
Brand Cream Cheese
1½ cups sugar
1 egg
1 teaspoon vanilla
2½ cups flour
⅓ cup cocoa
1 teaspoon baking powder
½ cup chopped pecans
½ cup drained chopped
maraschino cherries

Heat oven to 375°. Combine margarine, softened cream cheese and sugar; mix well. Stir in egg and vanilla. Add combined flour, cocoa and baking powder; mix well. Add nuts and cherries. Drop by teaspoonfuls onto greased baking sheet. Bake at 375°, 12 to 15 minutes. 5 to 5½ dozen.

Jeweled Spice Bars

1 8-ounce package Philadelphia
Brand Cream Cheese
½ cup margarine
1½ cups brown sugar, packed
1 egg
¼ cup honey
2 cups flour
1½ teaspoons baking powder
1 teaspoon salt
1 teaspoon cinnamon
1 teaspoon nutmeg
1 cup chopped nuts
1 cup chopped candied fruit
½ cup raisins
*   *   *
1⅓ cups sifted confectioners'
sugar
2 tablespoons milk
¼ teaspoon vanilla

Heat oven to 350°. Combine softened cream cheese, margarine, sugar and egg; mix until well blended. Stir in honey. Combine flour, baking powder, salt, cinnamon and nutmeg. Add nuts, candied fruit and raisins; toss lightly to coat fruit. Gradually add to cream cheese mixture. Pour into greased and floured 15½ x 10½-inch jelly roll pan. Bake at 350°, 30 to 35 minutes. Combine confectioners' sugar, milk and vanilla. Drizzle over warm bars; cool. Cut into 3 x 1-inch bars. 50 bars.

Bavarian Apple Torte

½ cup margarine
⅓ cup sugar
¼ teaspoon vanilla
1 cup flour
*   *   *
1 8-ounce package Philadelphia
Brand Cream Cheese, cubed
¼ cup sugar
1 egg
½ teaspoon vanilla
*   *   *
⅓ cup sugar
½ teaspoon cinnamon
4 cups sliced peeled apples
¼ cup sliced almonds

Heat oven to 450°. Cream margarine, sugar and vanilla. Blend in flour. Spread dough on bottom and 1½ inches high around sides of 9-inch springform pan. Combine softened cream cheese and sugar; mix well. Add egg and vanilla; mix. Pour into pastry-lined pan. Combine sugar and cinnamon. Toss apples in sugar mixture. Spoon apples over cream cheese layer; sprinkle with nuts. Bake at 450°, 10 minutes. Reduce temperature to 400°; continue baking 25 minutes. Loosen torte from rim of pan; cool before removing rim of pan. 8 to 10 servings.

Gala Gingerbread

1 package gingerbread mix
¾ cup sugar
3 tablespoons cornstarch
1 cup water
¼ cup lemon juice
1 egg yolk
Kraft Whipped Cream Cheese

Prepare gingerbread as directed on package. Combine sugar and cornstarch; blend in water and lemon juice. Cook until clear and thickened, stirring occasionally. Add small amount to slightly beaten egg yolk; return mixture to pan. Cook 2 to 3 minutes. Cut gingerbread in squares. Top each square with whipped cream cheese and lemon sauce. 8 to 10 servings.

Apple Cheddar Shortcake

2½ cups biscuit mix
1 cup (4 ounces) shredded
Cracker Barrel Brand Sharp
Natural Cheddar Cheese
⅔ cup milk
⅓ cup margarine, melted
* * *
¾ cup brown sugar, packed
3 tablespoons cornstarch
½ teaspoon cinnamon
¼ teaspoon salt
1 cup water
4 cups sliced, peeled apples
Heavy cream, whipped

Heat oven to 425°. Combine biscuit mix and cheese; stir in milk and margarine. Spread dough into two greased 8-inch layer pans; bake at 425°, 20 minutes. Combine brown sugar, cornstarch, cinnamon and salt. Stir in water; cook until clear and thickened. Add apples; cover and simmer until tender. Spoon half of apples over one layer. Top with second layer and remaining apples. Serve warm with whipped cream. 6 to 8 servings.

Maple Mincemeat Apples

6 large baking apples
1 cup mincemeat
¾ cup maple syrup
½ cup water
¼ teaspoon cinnamon
Kraft Whipped Cream Cheese

Heat oven to 375°. Core apples. Pare wide strip around each apple. Place apples in shallow baking pan. Fill centers with mincemeat. Combine syrup, water and cinnamon. Pour over apples; bake at 375°, 45 minutes or until tender, basting occasionally with syrup. Top with whipped cream cheese. 6 servings.

"Philly" Marble Cake

*1 8-ounce package Philadelphia
Brand Cream Cheese
1 cup margarine
1½ cups sugar
1½ teaspoons vanilla
3 eggs
2¼ cups sifted cake flour
1½ teaspoons baking powder
2 1-ounce squares unsweetened
chocolate, melted
½ teaspoon soda
Glaze*

Heat oven to 325°. Thoroughly blend softened cream cheese, margarine, sugar and vanilla. Add eggs, one at a time, mixing well after each addition. Gradually add flour sifted with baking powder; mix well. Reserve 2 cups batter. Add chocolate and soda to remaining batter, mixing well. Spoon chocolate and white batters alternately into greased and floured 10-inch bundt or tube pan. Cut through batter with knife several times for marble effect. Bake at 325°, 1 hour. Cool 5 minutes; remove from pan and glaze immediately. 16 to 18 servings.

Glaze

*2 tablespoons margarine
2 tablespoons milk
1½ cups sifted confectioners'
sugar
½ teaspoon vanilla*

Heat margarine and milk. Add sugar; beat until smooth. Stir in vanilla.

Cheddar Pear Cobbler

*2 1-pound cans pear halves
1 tablespoon sugar
2 tablespoons cornstarch
¼ teaspoon cinnamon
1 tablespoon lemon juice
* * *
1 cup flour
⅓ cup sugar
1½ teaspoons baking powder
½ teaspoon salt
1½ cups (6 ounces) shredded
Cracker Barrel Brand Sharp
Natural Cheddar Cheese
⅓ cup margarine, melted
¼ cup milk*

Heat oven to 425°. Drain pears, reserving syrup. Combine sugar, cornstarch and cinnamon in saucepan. Add syrup and lemon juice. Heat until syrup thickens; boil 1 minute. Remove from heat; add pears. Spoon pears and syrup into 9-inch square pan. Combine flour, sugar, baking powder, salt and cheese. Add margarine and milk; mix until blended. Spoon dough over pears. Bake at 425°, 25 to 30 minutes. 6 to 8 servings.

Good idea: This is especially good topped with vanilla ice cream or whipped cream.

Pears Picasso

8 pears
2 cups miniature marshmallows
2 tablespoons milk
1 8-ounce package Philadelphia
  Brand Cream Cheese
2 tablespoons brandy
½ cup heavy cream, whipped
Chocolate flavored topping

Peel pears and core from the bottom. Place pears in saucepan with enough water to cover. Cover and simmer 20 minutes or until tender; drain. Chill. Melt marshmallows with milk in double boiler; stir until smooth. Chill until thickened. Combine softened cream cheese and brandy, beating until well blended and fluffy. Whip in marshmallow mixture; fold in whipped cream. For each serving, place ½ cup cream cheese mixture in serving dish. Top with pear. Spoon chocolate flavored topping over pear before serving. 8 servings.

Peach Melba Metropolitan

Canned peach halves
Kraft Whipped Cream Cheese
Peach Melba Sauce

For each serving, place peach half in serving dish; top with whipped cream cheese and sauce.

Peach Melba Sauce

1 10-ounce package frozen
  raspberries, thawed
⅓ cup red currant jelly
2 tablespoons cornstarch

Drain berries; reserve juice. Add water, if necessary, to make ⅔ cup liquid. Combine juice, jelly and cornstarch in saucepan. Cook over medium heat until clear and thickened. Stir in raspberries. 1½ cups.

Chocolate Mint Royale

1 cup chocolate wafer crumbs
¼ cup chopped pecans
3 tablespoons margarine,
  melted
*   *   *   *
1 envelope unflavored gelatin
1 cup water
1 8-ounce package Philadelphia
  Brand Cream Cheese
1 cup sugar
1½ teaspoons vanilla
½ teaspoon peppermint extract
3 1-ounce squares semi-sweet
  chocolate, melted
1 cup heavy cream, whipped

Heat oven to 325°. Combine crumbs, nuts and margarine. Press onto bottom of 9-inch springform pan. Bake at 325°, 10 minutes. Soften gelatin in ½ cup water; add remaining water. Stir over low heat until gelatin is dissolved. Combine softened cream cheese, sugar, vanilla and peppermint extract, mixing until well blended. Stir in chocolate; gradually add gelatin. Chill until slightly thickened. Fold in whipped cream. Pour over crumbs; chill until firm. Garnish with additional whipped cream and pecan halves, if desired. 10 to 12 servings.

Fruit Fantasy

*1 1-pound 2-ounce package
refrigerated sugar cookie dough
1 8-ounce package Philadelphia
Brand Cream Cheese
⅓ cup sugar
½ teaspoon vanilla
Orange sections
Green grapes, cut in half
Banana slices
Strawberries, cut in half
¼ cup orange marmalade
1 tablespoon water*

Heat oven to 375°. Cut cookie dough into slices ⅛-inch thick. Line 14-inch pizza pan with cookie slices, overlapping slightly. Bake at 375°, 12 minutes. Cool. Combine softened cream cheese, sugar and vanilla, mixing until well blended. Spread mixture over cookie crust. Arrange fruit over cream cheese layer. Glaze with combined marmalade and water. Chill. Cut in wedges to serve. 10 to 12 servings.

Apple Turnovers

*2¼ cups flour
¼ teaspoon salt
⅔ cup shortening
1½ cups (6 ounces) shredded
Cracker Barrel Brand Sharp
Natural Cheddar Cheese
6 to 8 tablespoons water
¾ cup brown sugar, packed
1 teaspoon cinnamon
6 medium baking apples,
pared, cored
¼ cup margarine
Sweetened whipped cream*

Heat oven to 425°. Combine flour and salt. Cut in shortening until mixture resembles coarse crumbs; stir in cheese. Sprinkle with water while mixing lightly with a fork; form into ball. Divide into three equal portions. Roll each on lightly floured surface to 14 x 7-inch rectangle; cut into 7-inch squares. Combine brown sugar and cinnamon; fill apple centers, topping each with margarine. Sprinkle remaining brown sugar mixture over pastry. Place apple in each square. Fold corners to center; pinch together. Bake at 425°, 30 to 35 minutes. Top with whipped cream. 6 servings.

Princess Babas

*2 cups (1-pound can) apricot
halves
Honey
½ cup orange juice
3 tablespoons rum
6 individual sponge cakes
Slivered almonds, toasted
Coarse or granulated sugar
1 fresh pear, cut in thin
wedges
Kraft Whipped Cream Cheese*

Drain apricots, reserving syrup. Combine syrup, ¾ cup honey and orange juice; simmer 15 minutes. Add rum; reserve ¾ cup sauce. Spoon remaining sauce over cakes; chill. Coat nuts with honey; roll in sugar. Top cakes with fruit, whipped cream cheese and reserved sauce. Sprinkle with nuts. 6 servings.

Snow-capped Crisp

1 1-pound jar fruit salad
1 1-pound can apricot halves
1/4 teaspoon nutmeg
1/2 cup flour
1/2 cup brown sugar, packed
1/4 teaspoon salt
1/4 cup margarine
1/2 cup chopped walnuts
Kraft Whipped Cream Cheese

Heat oven to 400°. Drain fruit salad and apricots. Combine fruit salad, apricots and nutmeg in 10 x 6-inch baking dish. Combine flour, sugar and salt; cut in margarine until mixture resembles coarse crumbs. Stir in nuts; sprinkle over fruit. Bake at 400°, 15 minutes. Serve warm, topped with whipped cream cheese. 8 servings.

Blueberry Grunt

1 1-pound 5-ounce can
blueberry pie filling
1 cup sugar
3/4 cup flour
1/2 teaspoon cinnamon
1/4 teaspoon salt
1/3 cup margarine
Kraft Whipped Cream Cheese

Heat oven to 350°. Spoon pie filling into 10 x 6-inch baking dish. Combine sugar, flour, cinnamon and salt; cut in margarine until mixture resembles coarse crumbs. Sprinkle over pie filling. Bake at 350°, 45 minutes. Serve warm, topped with whipped cream cheese. 6 servings.

Cheddar Apple Dandy

6 cups sliced peeled apples
1/4 cup sugar
2 tablespoons flour
1 1/2 cups (6 ounces) shredded
Cracker Barrel Brand Sharp
Natural Cheddar Cheese
3/4 cup flour
1/4 cup sugar
1/2 teaspoon cinnamon
1/4 teaspoon salt
1/2 cup margarine

Heat oven to 375°. Combine apples, sugar, flour and 1 cup cheese. Place in greased 8-inch square pan. Combine flour, sugar, cinnamon and salt. Cut in margarine until mixture resembles coarse crumbs; sprinkle over apple mixture. Bake at 375°, 30 to 35 minutes. Top with remaining cheese; return to oven until cheese melts. 6 servings.

Dessert Sandwiches

Date-nut or Boston brown
bread, sliced
Kraft Whipped Cream Cheese
Orange marmalade or apricot
preserves

For each sandwich, spread slice of bread with whipped cream cheese; top with marmalade or preserves and second slice of bread.

Out-of-This-World Dessert

¼ cup cold water
1 envelope unflavored gelatin
½ cup boiling water
1 cup heavy cream
2 tablespoons sugar
1 8-ounce package Philadelphia Brand Cream Cheese, cubed
1 cup (4 ounces) shredded Cracker Barrel Brand Sharp Natural Cheddar Cheese
2 tablespoons Kraft Cold Pack Blue Cheese
Sliced apples
Sliced pears
Green grapes

Pour cold water into blender container; add gelatin and let stand a few minutes to soften. Add boiling water; mix on low speed until gelatin is dissolved. Using high speed, blend in cream and sugar. Gradually add remaining ingredients except fruit, mixing until well blended. Pour into 1-quart mold. Chill until firm. Unmold and serve with fruit. 8 to 10 servings.
Nice to know: A 9-inch square pan may be used.

"Philly" Pastry

1 3-ounce package Philadelphia Brand Cream Cheese
½ cup margarine
1 cup flour
⅛ teaspoon salt

Combine softened cream cheese and margarine; mix until well blended. Add flour and salt; mix well. Form into ball; chill overnight. Heat oven to 450°. Roll pastry to 11-inch circle on lightly floured surface. Place in 9-inch pie plate. Flute edge; prick with fork. Bake at 450°, 12 to 15 minutes. 1 9-inch pastry shell.
Nice to know: For tart shells, bake at 450°, 8 to 10 minutes. Makes 12 to 14 tart shells.

Chocolate "Philly" Mousse

1 4-ounce package chocolate pudding and pie filling mix
1¾ cups milk
1 teaspoon instant coffee
1 8-ounce package Philadelphia Brand Cream Cheese, cubed

Combine pudding mix, milk and instant coffee in saucepan. Cook over medium heat until mixture comes to full boil, stirring constantly. Add cream cheese; beat until blended. Pour into 1-quart mold. Place waxed paper on surface; chill until set. Unmold; garnish with whipped cream, if desired. 8 to 10 servings.
Another way: Substitute 2 tablespoons brandy or white crème de menthe for instant coffee.

Chocolate "Philly" Fudge

*4 cups sifted confectioners'
sugar*
*1 8-ounce package Philadelphia
Brand Cream Cheese*
½ cup chopped nuts
*4 1-ounce squares unsweetened
chocolate, melted*
1 teaspoon vanilla
Dash of salt

Gradually add sugar to softened cream cheese, mixing until well blended. Stir in remaining ingredients. Press into greased 8-inch square pan. Chill; cut into squares. Garnish with additional nuts, if desired. About 1½ pounds.

Other ways: Peppermint "Philly" Fudge—omit nuts and vanilla; add few drops peppermint extract. Sprinkle with ½ cup crushed peppermint candy. Coconut "Philly" Fudge—omit nuts; add 1 cup shredded coconut. Garnish with additional coconut, if desired. Cherry "Philly" Fudge—omit nuts; add one 4-ounce jar maraschino cherries, drained and chopped. Garnish with whole cherries, if desired.

Chocolate "Philly" Frosting

*1 8-ounce package Philadelphia
Brand Cream Cheese*
1 tablespoon milk
1 teaspoon vanilla
Dash of salt
*5 cups sifted confectioners'
sugar*
*3 1-ounce squares
unsweetened chocolate,
melted*

Combine softened cream cheese, milk, vanilla and salt, mixing until well blended. Gradually add sugar. Stir in chocolate. Frosts an 8 or 9-inch layer cake.

Chocolate Velvet Cream

*1½ cups chocolate wafer
crumbs*
⅓ cup margarine, melted
* * *
*1 8-ounce package Philadelphia
Brand Cream Cheese*
½ cup sugar
1 teaspoon vanilla
2 eggs, separated
*1 6-ounce package semi-sweet
chocolate pieces, melted*
1 cup heavy cream, whipped
¾ cup chopped pecans

Heat oven to 325°. Combine crumbs and margarine. Press into 13 x 9-inch baking pan or 9-inch springform pan. Bake at 325°, 10 minutes. Combine softened cream cheese, ¼ cup sugar and vanilla, mixing until well blended. Stir in beaten egg yolks and chocolate. Beat egg whites until soft peaks form. Gradually beat in remaining ¼ cup sugar; fold into chocolate mixture. Fold in whipped cream and nuts. Pour over crumbs; freeze. Garnish with shaved chocolate or whipped cream before serving, if desired. 10 to 12 servings.

Pineapple "Philly" Pie

⅓ cup sugar
1 tablespoon cornstarch
1 cup (8½-ounce can)
crushed pineapple,
undrained
1 9-inch unbaked pastry
shell

* * *

1 8-ounce package
Philadelphia Brand Cream
Cheese
½ cup sugar
½ teaspoon salt
2 eggs
½ cup milk
½ teaspoon vanilla
¼ cup chopped pecans

Combine sugar and cornstarch; add pineapple. Cook, stirring constantly, until clear and thickened. Cool; spread on bottom of pastry shell. Heat oven to 400°. Combine softened cream cheese, sugar and salt, mixing until well blended. Add eggs, one at a time, mixing well after each addition. Blend in milk and vanilla. Pour over pineapple mixture; sprinkle with nuts. Bake at 400°, 15 min-

utes; reduce temperature to 325° and continue baking 40 minutes. Cool before serving. Garnish with pineapple slices and pecan halves, if desired.

Paradise Pumpkin Pie

1 8-ounce package
Philadelphia Brand Cream
Cheese
¼ cup sugar
½ teaspoon vanilla
1 egg
1 9-inch unbaked pastry
shell

* * *

1¼ cups canned or cooked
pumpkin
½ cup sugar
1 teaspoon cinnamon
¼ teaspoon ginger
¼ teaspoon nutmeg
Dash of salt
1 cup evaporated milk
2 eggs, slightly beaten

Heat oven to 350°. Combine softened cream cheese, sugar and vanilla, mixing until well blended. Add egg; mix well. Spread onto bottom of pastry shell. Combine remaining ingredients; mix well. Carefully pour over cream cheese mixture. Bake at 350°, 1 hour and 5 minutes or until done. Cool. Brush with maple syrup and garnish with nuts, if desired.

Cheddar-Crust Apple Pie

1½ cups flour
Dash of salt
½ cup shortening
1½ cups (6 ounces) shredded
Cracker Barrel Brand Sharp
Natural Cheddar Cheese
4 to 6 tablespoons water
* * *

½ cup sugar
2 tablespoons flour
¼ teaspoon cinnamon
6 cups sliced peeled apples
2 tablespoons margarine

Heat oven to 425°. Combine flour and salt; cut in shortening until mixture resembles coarse crumbs. Stir in cheese. Sprinkle with water while mixing lightly with a fork; form into ball. Divide dough in half. Roll one part to 11-inch circle on lightly floured surface. Place in 9-inch pie plate. Combine sugar, flour and cinnamon. Mix with apples. Place mixture in pie shell; dot with margarine. Roll out remainder of dough to 11-inch circle; place over apples. Seal edges of crust and flute. Cut slits in top of pastry. Bake at 425°, 35 minutes.

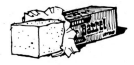

Praline Cheese Cake

1 cup graham cracker crumbs
3 tablespoons sugar
3 tablespoons margarine,
melted
* * *

3 8-ounce packages
Philadelphia Brand Cream
Cheese
1¼ cups dark brown sugar,
packed
2 tablespoons flour
3 eggs
1½ teaspoons vanilla
½ cup finely chopped pecans

Heat oven to 350°. Combine crumbs, sugar and margarine; press onto bottom of 9-inch springform pan. Bake at 350°, 10 minutes. Combine softened cream cheese, sugar and flour, mixing at medium speed on electric mixer until well blended. Add eggs, one at a time, mixing well after each addition. Blend in vanilla and nuts. Pour mixture over crumbs. Bake at 350°, 50 to 55 minutes. Loosen cake from rim of pan; cool before removing rim of pan. Chill. Brush with maple syrup and garnish with pecan halves, if desired. 10 to 12 servings.

Opposite: Praline Cheese Cake

Cream Cheese Pie

2 8-ounce packages
Philadelphia Brand Cream
Cheese
¾ cup sugar
2 teaspoons lemon juice
½ teaspoon vanilla
3 eggs
1 9-inch graham cracker
crust

Heat oven to 325°. Combine softened cream cheese, sugar, lemon juice and vanilla, mixing until well blended. Add eggs, one at a time, mixing well after each addition. Pour into crust; bake at 325°, 30 minutes. Chill.

Easy Deep Dish Apple Pie

2 1-pound cans apple pie
filling
½ cup raisins
1 cup (4 ounces) shredded
Cracker Barrel Brand
Sharp Natural Cheddar
Cheese
1 8-ounce can refrigerated
crescent dinner rolls
2 tablespoons sugar
¼ teaspoon cinnamon

Heat oven to 375°. Spoon pie filling into 12 x 8-inch baking dish. Sprinkle with raisins and cheese. Unroll both halves of refrigerated dough into flat rectangular sheets. Fit to cover baking dish. Combine sugar and cinnamon; sprinkle evenly over dough. Bake at 375°, 25 minutes. Top with cheese slices, if desired. 8 servings.

Chocolate Cloud Pie

1¼ cups chocolate wafer
crumbs
¼ cup margarine, melted
2 tablespoons sugar
*   *   *
2 8-ounce packages
Philadelphia Brand Cream
Cheese
¾ cup brown sugar, packed
1 teaspoon vanilla
1 6-ounce package semi-sweet
chocolate pieces, melted
2 eggs

Heat oven to 325°. Combine crumbs, margarine and sugar. Press onto bottom and sides of 9-inch pie plate. Bake at 325°, 10 minutes. Combine softened cream cheese, sugar and vanilla, mixing until well blended. Stir in chocolate. Add eggs, one at a time, mixing well after each addition. Pour over crumbs. Bake at 325°, 35 minutes. Cool before serving.

Fresh Strawberry Glacé Pie

1 8-ounce package
Philadelphia Brand Cream
Cheese
2 tablespoons milk
2 tablespoons sugar
¼ teaspoon almond extract
1 9-inch baked pastry shell
3 cups fresh strawberries,
halved
¼ cup sugar
1 tablespoon cornstarch
½ cup water
Few drops red food
coloring

Combine softened cream cheese, milk, 2 tablespoons sugar and extract, mixing until well blended. Spread cream cheese mixture on bottom of pastry shell; cover with 2¾ cups strawberries. Combine ¼ cup sugar and cornstarch in saucepan. Add water and remaining strawberries, mashed. Stir mixture over medium heat until clear and thickened; cool. Pour over strawberries; chill.

Sun-Sational Cheese Cake

1 cup graham cracker crumbs
3 tablespoons sugar
3 tablespoons margarine,
melted
* * *
3 8-ounce packages
Philadelphia Brand Cream
Cheese
1 cup sugar
3 tablespoons flour
2 tablespoons lemon juice
1 tablespoon grated lemon
rind
½ teaspoon vanilla
4 eggs (1 separated)
* * *
¾ cup sugar

2 tablespoons cornstarch
½ cup water
¼ cup lemon juice

Heat oven to 325°. Combine crumbs, sugar and margarine. Press onto bottom of 9-inch springform pan. Bake at 325°, 10 minutes. Increase oven temperature to 450°. Combine softened cream cheese, sugar, flour, lemon juice, lemon rind and vanilla, mixing at medium speed on electric mixer until well blended. Add 3 eggs, one at a time, mixing well after each addition. Beat in remaining egg white; reserve egg yolk for glaze. Pour mixture over crumbs; bake at 450°, 10 minutes. Reduce temperature to 250°; continue baking for 30 minutes. Loosen cake from rim of pan; cool before removing rim of pan. Combine sugar and cornstarch; add water and lemon juice. Cook until clear and thickened, stirring occasionally. Add small amount to slightly beaten egg yolk; return mixture to pan and cook a few minutes longer. Cool slightly. Spoon over cheese cake; chill until firm. Garnish with lemon slices, if desired. 10 to 12 servings.

Crescent City Cheese Cake

1 cup graham cracker crumbs
3 tablespoons sugar
3 tablespoons margarine,
   melted
*   *   *
2 8-ounce packages
Philadelphia Brand Cream
   Cheese
½ cup sugar
1 tablespoon lemon juice
1 teaspoon grated lemon
   rind
3 eggs
1 cup dairy sour cream
*   *   *
1 10-ounce package frozen
   strawberries, thawed
¼ cup water
1 tablespoon cornstarch

Heat oven to 350°. Combine crumbs, sugar and margarine; press onto bottom of 9-inch springform pan. Combine softened cream cheese, sugar, lemon juice and rind, mixing at medium speed on electric mixer until well blended. Add eggs, one at a time, mixing well after each addition. Blend in sour cream. Pour mixture over crumbs; bake at 350°, 55 minutes. Loosen cake from rim of pan; cool before removing rim of pan. Drain strawberries, reserving ⅓ cup juice. Combine juice from strawberries, water and cornstarch. Cook until clear and thickened, stirring occasionally; cool. Add strawberries. Spoon over cake; chill. 10 to 12 servings.

Creamy Cocoa Cheese Cake

1 cup graham cracker crumbs
3 tablespoons sugar
3 tablespoons margarine,
   melted
*   *   *
2 8-ounce packages
Philadelphia Brand Cream
   Cheese
¾ cup sugar
⅓ cup cocoa
1 teaspoon vanilla
2 eggs
*   *   *
1 cup dairy sour cream
2 tablespoons sugar
1 teaspoon vanilla

Heat oven to 375°. Combine crumbs, sugar and margarine. Press onto bottom and sides of 9-inch springform pan. Combine softened cream cheese, sugar, cocoa and vanilla, mixing at medium speed on electric mixer until well blended. Add eggs, one at a time, mixing well after each addition. Pour mixture over crumbs. Bake at 375°, 30 minutes. Remove from oven; cool for 15 minutes. Increase oven temperature to 425°. Combine sour cream, sugar and vanilla. Carefully spread over baked filling. Return to oven; bake at 425°, 10 minutes. Loosen cake from rim of pan; cool before removing rim of pan. Chill. 10 to 12 servings.

Cool and Creamy Cheese Cake

1 cup graham cracker crumbs
¼ cup sugar
¼ cup margarine, melted
*   *   *
1 envelope unflavored gelatin
¼ cup water
1 8-ounce package Philadelphia
Brand Cream Cheese
½ cup sugar
Dash of salt
¼ cup lemon juice
¾ cup milk
1 cup heavy cream, whipped
Fresh or frozen peaches,
strawberries or blueberries

Combine crumbs, sugar and margarine; press onto bottom of 9-inch springform pan. Soften gelatin in water; stir over low heat until dissolved. Combine softened cream cheese, sugar and salt, mixing at medium speed on electric mixer until well blended. Gradually add lemon juice, milk and gelatin; chill until slightly thickened. Fold in whipped cream; pour over crust. Chill until firm. Top with fruit just before serving. 8 to 10 servings.

Minted Chocolate Freeze

1¼ cups graham cracker
crumbs
¼ cup sugar
⅓ cup margarine, melted
1 1-ounce square unsweetened
chocolate, melted
*   *   *
1 8-ounce package Philadelphia
Brand Cream Cheese
¾ cup brown sugar, packed
¼ teaspoon peppermint extract
1 6-ounce package semi-sweet
chocolate pieces, melted
2 eggs, separated
1 cup heavy cream, whipped
½ cup chopped pecans

Combine crumbs and sugar; stir in margarine and chocolate. Press onto bottom of 9-inch square pan; chill. Combine softened cream cheese, ½ cup sugar and peppermint extract, mixing until well blended. Stir in chocolate and egg yolks. Beat egg whites until soft peaks form. Gradually beat in remaining ¼ cup sugar; fold into chocolate mixture. Fold in whipped cream and nuts. Freeze. 8 to 10 servings.

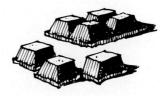

Cheese Cookery for a Crowd

Family reunion, church supper, a large gathering of friends for a special occasion—whatever the reason, you'll someday find yourself preparing food for a crowd. Here are recipes for delectable, easy, cooked-in-quantity dishes.

Meatloaf Italiano

4 pounds ground beef
4 cups fresh bread crumbs
2 cups water
1 cup chopped onion
½ cup (2 ounces) Kraft Grated
  Parmesan Cheese
4 eggs, beaten
1 tablespoon salt
½ teaspoon pepper

*   *   *

2 8-ounce cans tomato sauce
1 teaspoon oregano
2 cups (8 ounces) shredded
Kraft Natural Low Moisture
Part-Skim Mozzarella Cheese

Heat oven to 375°. Combine meat, bread crumbs, water, onion, Parmesan cheese, eggs and seasonings; mix lightly. Press 5¾ cups of mixture into each of two 13 x 9-inch baking pans. Bake at 375°, 30 minutes; pour off drippings. Combine tomato sauce and oregano; pour 1 cup of mixture over each meatloaf. Sprinkle each meatloaf with 1 cup of Mozzarella cheese; return to oven for 30 minutes. 20 to 24 servings.

Grills for the Group

3 12-ounce cans luncheon meat,
  cut in chunks
¼ cup chopped green pepper
¼ cup chopped onion

4 cups (1 pound) shredded
Cracker Barrel Brand Sharp
Natural Cheddar Cheese
¾ cup salad dressing
⅓ cup sweet pickle relish
½ teaspoon pepper
60 slices sandwich bread
Soft margarine

Grind together luncheon meat, green pepper and onion. Add cheese, salad dressing, pickle relish and pepper; mix well. Chill. For each sandwich, cover 1 slice of bread with ¼ cup meat mixture; top with second slice of bread. Spread bread with margarine; grill on both sides until golden brown. 30 sandwiches.

Nice to know: For cold sandwiches, spread bread with salad dressing; top with lettuce and meat mixture.

Mission Macaroni Salad

1 pound elbow macaroni,
  cooked, drained
1 pound Old English Sharp
Pasteurized Process Cheese,
  cubed
¾ cup sliced ripe olives
¼ cup sliced green onion
1 4-ounce can pimiento,
  drained, chopped
1½ cups salad dressing
½ teaspoon salt
¼ teaspoon pepper

Combine macaroni, cheese, olives, onion and pimiento; mix lightly. Add combined salad dressing and seasonings; mix well. Chill. 24 ½-cup servings.

Lasagne Largo

3 pounds ground beef
1½ cups chopped onion
3 1-pound cans tomatoes
4 6-ounce cans tomato paste
2 cups water
2 tablespoons oregano
1 teaspoon pepper
½ teaspoon garlic salt

*　*　*

1 pound lasagne noodles,
cooked, drained
4 6-ounce packages Kraft
Natural Low Moisture
Part-Skim Mozzarella Cheese
Slices
1½ pounds Velveeta Pasteurized
Process Cheese Spread, sliced
1½ cups (6 ounces) Kraft
Grated Parmesan Cheese

Heat oven to 350°. Brown meat; drain. Add onion; cook until tender. Stir in tomatoes, tomato paste, water and seasonings; cover and simmer 30 minutes. In each of two 13 x 9-inch baking pans, layer half of noodles, meat sauce and cheeses; repeat layers. Bake at 350°, 35 to 40 minutes. Let stand 15 minutes before serving. 24 servings.
Nice to know: This dish may be covered and refrigerated overnight; remove cover and bake at 350°, 1 hour.

Mashed Potatoes Parmesan

1 cup (4 ounces) Kraft Grated
Parmesan Cheese
¾ cup chopped green onion
12 cups hot seasoned mashed
potatoes

Add cheese and green onion to mashed potatoes; mix well. 24 ½-cup servings.

Snow-capped Tomatoes

12 tomatoes, cut in half
6 cups hot mashed potatoes
1½ cups (6 ounces) shredded
Cracker Barrel Brand Sharp
Natural Cheddar Cheese
¼ cup chopped parsley

Heat oven to 450°. Top each tomato half with ¼ cup potatoes and 1 tablespoon cheese. Sprinkle with parsley. Bake at 450°, 15 minutes. 24 servings.

Baked Chicken Salad

12 cups diced cooked chicken
6 cups sliced celery
4 cups (1 pound) shredded
Cracker Barrel Brand Sharp
Natural Cheddar Cheese
¼ cup chopped onion
¼ cup lemon juice
4 teaspoons salt
½ teaspoon pepper
2 cups mayonnaise
4 medium tomatoes, sliced
4 cups potato chips, crushed

Heat oven to 350°. Combine chicken, celery, 2 cups cheese, onion, lemon juice, seasonings and mayonnaise; toss lightly. Spoon into two 13 x 9-inch baking pans. Top with tomato slices. Bake at 350°, 35 to 40 minutes. Combine remaining cheese and potato chips; sprinkle over chicken mixture. Return to oven until cheese melts. 24 ¾-cup servings.

Cheddary Potato Salad

12 cups diced cooked potatoes
2 cups sliced celery
8 hard-cooked eggs, chopped
4 cups (1 pound) shredded
Cracker Barrel Brand Sharp
Natural Cheddar Cheese
¾ cup sliced green onion
2 cups salad dressing
1 tablespoon prepared mustard
1 tablespoon salt
¼ teaspoon pepper

Combine potatoes, celery, eggs, cheese and onion; mix lightly. Add combined salad dressing, mustard and seasonings; mix lightly. Chill. 18 to 24 servings.

"Philly" Waldorf Salad

2 8-ounce packages
Philadelphia Brand Cream
Cheese
½ cup orange juice
2 tablespoons sugar
2 tablespoons grated orange
rind
12 cups diced unpeeled apples
4 cups chopped celery
1 cup coarsely chopped pecans

Combine softened cream cheese, orange juice, sugar and orange rind, mixing until well blended. Combine apples, celery and nuts. Add dressing; toss lightly. Chill. 24 ¾-cup servings.

Festive Orange Salad

2 1-pound cans peach slices
4 3-ounce packages orange
flavored gelatin
4 cups boiling water
4 8-ounce packages
Philadelphia Brand Cream
Cheese
·2 cups cold water
2 teaspoons almond extract
1 cup maraschino cherries,
cut in half

Drain peach slices, reserving 2 cups syrup. Dissolve gelatin in boiling water. Gradually add to softened cream cheese, blending until smooth. Stir in cold water, peach syrup and almond extract. Chill until slightly thickened. Fold in fruit. Pour into two 8-inch square pans. Chill until firm. 24 servings.

Cherry Cheese Delight

*2¼ cups graham cracker
crumbs
⅔ cup margarine, melted*

* * *

*2 8-ounce packages
Philadelphia Brand Cream
Cheese
1½ cups sifted confectioners'
sugar
2 tablespoons milk
2 teaspoons almond extract
1 cup chopped pecans
2 cups heavy cream
2 1-pound 6-ounce cans cherry
pie filling*

Combine crumbs and margarine. Press into 15½ x 10½-inch jelly roll pan. Combine softened cream cheese, 1 cup sugar, milk and 1 teaspoon almond extract; mix until well blended. Spread mixture on graham cracker crust; sprinkle with nuts. Combine cream and remaining sugar; whip until stiff. Spread whipped cream over nuts. Combine pie filling and remaining almond extract; spread over whipped cream. Chill. 24 servings.

Chocolate Velvet Cream

*3 cups chocolate wafer crumbs
⅔ cup margarine, melted*

* * *

*2 8-ounce packages
Philadelphia Brand Cream
Cheese
1 cup sugar
2 teaspoons vanilla
4 eggs, separated
1 12-ounce package semi-sweet
chocolate pieces, melted
2 cups heavy cream, whipped
1½ cups chopped pecans*

Heat oven to 325°. Combine crumbs and margarine. Press 1½ cups of crumb mixture into each of two 13 x 9-inch baking pans. Bake at 325°, 10 minutes. Combine softened cream cheese, ½ cup sugar and vanilla, mixing until well blended. Stir in beaten egg yolks and chocolate. Beat egg whites until soft peaks form. Gradually beat in remaining ½ cup sugar; fold into chocolate mixture. Fold in whipped cream and nuts. Pour 6 cups of chocolate mixture into each pan. Freeze. 24 to 30 servings.

Perfect Partners:
Cheese and Wine

Beyond memory, from one end of the earth to the other, people have been eating cheese and drinking wine, combining them into a simple, wholesome snack or calling the two in combination a full meal. Cheese with wine is hearty fare—depending on the country, a peasant will add a chunk of crusty bread and, perhaps, a handful of olives or of nuts in the shell; sometimes a green salad will accompany the cheese-wine-bread meal, refuting those who say that the sharpness of oil-and-vinegar dressing "fights" the flavor and aroma of wine; sometimes a piece of fruit—with more cheese—will round off the repast, a juicy pear, perhaps, or a crisp apple.

Those of us who have tried this kind of cheese-and-wine meal know what great eating really can be; those who consider such a meal not worth considering have missed one of the world's great gastronomical treats.

What Wine with What Cheese?

A red wine, some experts say, goes best with most kinds of cheese. But suit your own taste. There once was a great mystique surrounding the buying, serving and drinking of wine. In those days, each wine had to have its own "proper" glass; wines of different kinds had to follow a prescribed order of service throughout a meal that often offered seven different wines to accompany as many different courses.

Now happily—and much more simply—we let our taste be our guide when we choose a cheese and then choose a wine to go with it. Most of the variously shaped wine glasses have disappeared, too, and we serve many kinds of wine in a simple, all-purpose, tulip-shaped stemmed glass that serves for any wine, any occasion.

Good Taste, Good Sense

A simple rule for choosing cheese and wine to go together: Trust yourself, your taste, your common sense. It's very unlikely that you'll even think of partnering Limburger or Lager Käse with champagne or, at the other extreme, Philadelphia Brand Cream Cheese and fresh strawberries for dessert with a young and harsh Chianti. In between such limits of absurdity, let your taste and your good sense tell you what goes with what to suit *you*.

Here, to get you started on your cheese-and-wine thinking are some combinations that seem to have a particular affinity.

Camembert: Try a hearty red wine—perhaps a Pinot Noir or any of the other Burgundies or a Cabernet Sauvignon. This lovely, creamy cheese may also be served for dessert, with crackers and/or with fruit; in that case, serve a dessert wine.

Swiss and Gruyère: For these sweet, nutlike flavors, choose a white table wine—a Chablis or a sauterne, perhaps, or one of the Rhine wines or any of the fine American white wines. Champagne goes well with these cheeses, too—but doesn't champagne go well with just about everything?

Roquefort and Blue: Sharp and tangy in flavor, these cheeses, with their handsome blue-green veins, make perfect partners for sturdy red wines—a good, robust Burgundy or one of the Bordeaux wines or their American cousins. For a change, try a nutty dry sherry with these cheeses.

All the Cheddars: These range in flavor from mild to extra sharp. California's great Zinfandel or any rosé wine goes well with all the Cheddars except for the sharpest. With those, choose a Burgundy—perhaps a Beaujolais—or a sturdy Italian Chianti.

Provolone and Mozzarella: Both are soft, mild and smooth—provolone sometimes has a smoky flavor. Good Italian Chianti is an excellent choice. But rosé wines and white wines go well with these, too.

Edam and Gouda: The good "cannonball" cheeses make a fine marriage with Cabernet Sauvignon or do equally well with a sweeter, dessert-type wine, such as a rich port.

Cream Cheese and Neufchatel: Creamy, mild in flavor, these two are favorites of everyone, even those incredible few who say, "I don't like cheese." Serve with dessert wines—port or a cream sherry—or a sparkling wine.

Brick, Muenster and Monterey Jack: These are reasonably mild, yet each has a distinctive flavor. Rosés complement them beautifully. So does California's Gamay Beaujolais. Or experiment with a white wine of the Rhine type for a totally different flavor combination.

Cheese and Wine Tasting

Cheese and wine fit the modern mode of entertaining, whether formal or informal. In selecting cheese for a tasting, make a selection that offers a variety of flavors —from mild to sharp—and a blend of textures from creamy smooth to firm. Take advantage of the color and shape contrasts available in the world of cheeses.

Tips on serving cheese:

Temperature—cheese should be served at room temperature (remove from refrigerator an hour before serving) for greatest enjoyment.

Tasting—the more delicately flavored, mild cheeses should be sampled before the sharper cheeses.

Quantity—allow ¼ to ½ pound per person. The more types of cheese offered, the more of each cheese is required to provide an adequate sampling.

Tips on serving wine:

Temperature—wines vary in proper serving temperatures. Generally appetizer wines, white table wines, rosés and sparkling wines are chilled (an hour in the refrigerator is enough). Red wines are served at room temperature, and should be opened an hour before serving. (Open the wine when you remove the cheese from the refrigerator.)

Tasting—pour wines into clear glasses. Provide a clean glass for each wine, if possible. Or have a pitcher of water handy and a receptacle for rinsing glasses. Taste the dry wines before sweet wines, whites before reds.

Quantity—a fifth of wine gives about 15 tastings. Allow about one-half bottle per person. A tasting of wine is between 1 and 2 ounces, a normal serving 4 to 6 ounces.

Index